Ancient Peoples and Places

FINLAND

General Editor

DR. GLYN DANIEL

ABOUT THE AUTHOR

Ella Kivikoski was a staff member of the Helsinki National Museum from 1933 to 1948, serving as Keeper of the Archaeological Department during her last two years. She became a Lecturer in Archaeology at the University of Helsinki in 1941 and was appointed Professor of Archaeology in 1948. Author of several books and a frequent contributor to learned journals, Professor Kivikoski is currently President of Finland's Archaeological Society and a member of the Finnish Academy of Science and Letters.

Ancient Peoples and Places

FINLAND

Ella Kivikoski

66 PHOTOGRAPHS
16 LINE DRAWINGS
13 MAPS
1 TABLE

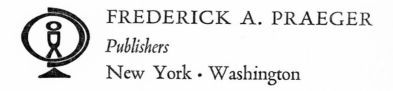

FREDERICK A. PRAEGER
Publishers
New York · Washington

THIS IS VOLUME FIFTY-THREE IN THE SERIES

Ancient Peoples and Places

GENERAL EDITOR: DR. GLYN DANIEL

This book was adapted by the author specifically for the Ancient Peoples and Places series from her Suomen Esihistoria *(volume I in the series* Suomen Historia*) published by* Werner Söderström Osakeyhtiö, Helsinki *in 1961. It was translated from the Swedish by Alan Binns.*

BOOKS THAT MATTER

*Published in the United States of America in 1967
by Frederick A. Praeger, Inc., Publishers,
111, Fourth Avenue, New York 3, N.Y. 10003*
*© Ella Kivikoski 1967
Library of Congress Catalog Card Number: 66–11423
Printed in Holland*

CONTENTS

5

ILLUSTRATIONS

7

8

Introduction

THE ORIGIN of the Finnish people has always fascinated students of their history, and the view that they were originally immigrants to Finland from the common home of the Finno-Ugrian peoples has always been the prevailing one. Folk-tales, sagas and place-names were used to trace this development in the past; nowadays it is principally philological and archaeological evidence which is used, and since true archaeology in Finland began, it has become possible to lay a firm foundation for the prehistory of the land and his people.

Scientific archaeology, in Finland as elsewhere, was preceded by a collector's interest in antiquities. Already during the Great Age of Sweden-Finland, the state had begun to take note of antiquities, and some of the measures for their conservation extended to Finland. The Collegium Antiquitatis, founded in 1667, instructed parish clergy to prepare an index of noteworthy remains in their parishes, and about twenty such returns came from Finland. Very few of the remains described were prehistoric. The local descriptions published by the Academy in Turku during the eighteenth century do however contain some accounts of prehistoric finds and by the end of the century public interest in the country's prehistory had increased. Students of the Academy carried this interest with them, and particularly in Ostrobothnia many priests collected antiquities, and some even undertook minor excavations. There was no question of course of scientific consideration of the finds; the basic three periods of prehistory were not yet established, and no value as source material was attributed to objects regarded simply as curiosities.

Scientific archaeology in Finland began in the middle of the nineteenth century, when J. R. Aspelin devoted himself to it. He published a number of works, mainly on Finno-Ugric antiquities in Russia, and on Finnish prehistory also, but his most important contribution was as an organizer of archaeological research in Finland. On his initiative the Archaeological Society of Finland *(Suomen Muinaismuistoyhdistys)* was started in 1870. Its publications, *Suomen Museo, Finskt Museum,* and *Suomen Muinais⁄ muistoyhdistyksen Aikakauskirja,* cover work done on Finnish pre⁄ history. As Government Archaeologist, Aspelin played a decisive part in the protection of antiquities and the foundation of the National Museum.

In the early years of the twentieth century Julius Ailio made a special study of the Stone Age, Alfred Hackman of the early Iron Age, work which remains valid after half a century; and A. M. Tallgren (first holder of the chair in Finnish and Scan⁄ dinavian archaeology established at Helsinki in 1921) of the East European Bronze Age. Many others could be named, as the Bibliography on page 157 shows. This book is an attempt to present the picture of Finnish prehistory which their work has drawn. Future researches will enrich this picture and prob⁄ ably alter it, but this is how it seems today.

E.K.

CHAPTER I

The Land Takes Shape

Fig. 1

THE DEVELOPMENT of Finland's history and prehistory was determined by its northerly latitude. The country extends from 60°N to 70°N into the Arctic Circle and towards the Polar area. In the east and south-east it is connected with the Eurasian land mass, and in the north-west with north Scandinavia, but to the west and south it fronts on the Baltic and its two arms, the Gulf of Finland and the Gulf of Bothnia. A nineteenth-century Finnish poet, Zachris Topelius uses a poetic term for Finland, 'the daughter of the sea' or 'the daughter of the Baltic'; he is referring to the rising of the land since the Ice Age which is still going on in the northern Baltic lands, and has given Finland its present form. As Topelius observes, the Baltic by this means has given her daughter another dukedom every century.

Fig. 2

During the Ice Age, which began about a million years ago, ice covered the whole of northern Europe, central Europe was a treeless tundra as far as the north coast of the Mediterranean, and southern Europe a region of coniferous forest. The cold was not continuous, and geologists distinguish three or four glaciations separated by warmer periods with a climate like that of the present-day. The inland ice at its most extensive covered more than half our hemisphere and during the last glaciation Finland, Scandinavia and a large area south of the Baltic were covered. The final thaw began about 16,000 BC, and after this the ice retreated northwards in stages. Finland began to emerge from the ice about 10,000 BC, and was completely free from it about 3000 years later. About 8000 BC the Salpausselkä ridges were formed, a system running east/west over the whole of south Finland, and after this the thaw proceeded rapidly. These dates are based on geological calculations mainly of stratified clays, and are con-

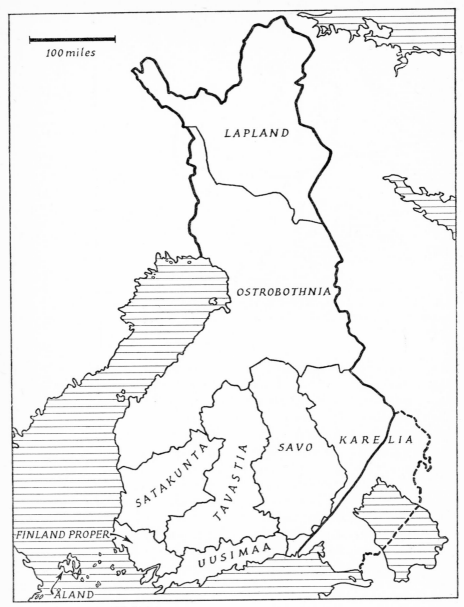

Fig. 1   The provinces of Finland

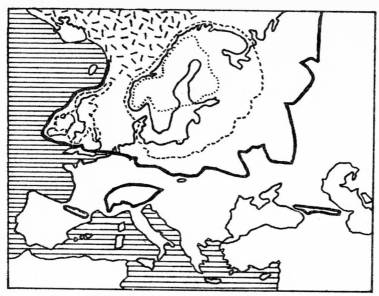

Fig. 2 The Ice Age in Europe. The thick black line marks the ice cover at its greatest, the broken line that of the final glaciation, and the dotted line that at the Salpausselkä stage. After Matti Sauramo

firmed by the results of carbon 14 dating. Ice has been decisive in forming the present face of Finland, carving hollows in the rock or polishing it, raising ridges and scarps from moraines. When the hollows filled with water the tens of thousands of lakes were formed which with the miles of forest are characteristic of our landscape. The countryside is in general flat, but the surface is irregular, and it slopes up to the north-east.

The emergence of Finland from the sea was one of many changes in the Baltic in these millennia. The melting ice formed the so-called Baltic ice-sea, which later, when central Sweden was freed from its corner of ice, flowed out through the broad sound formed over central Sweden. At the stage when the waters of the Baltic were at the same level as the ocean it is referred to as the Yoldia sea (8000–7300 BC) after a salt-water snail *Yoldia arcti-*

Fig. 3

15

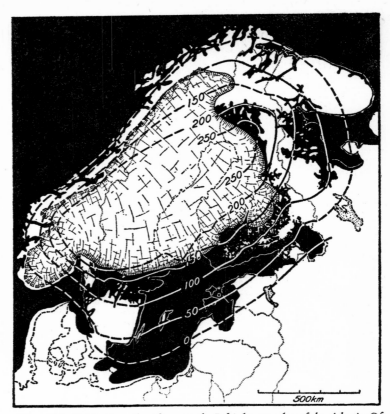

Fig. 3 The Yoldia Sea. About 8000 BC the Baltic became a bay of the Atlantic. Of Finland there was only a group of islands, which marked the later Salpausselkä. After Matti Sauramo

ca. The map shows the belt of islands in south Finland which formed the Salpausselkä ridges.

As the land continued to rise, the channel to the sea was cut, and the Baltic became a huge lake, the Ancylus sea, named after a freshwater snail *Ancylus fluviatilis.* The water sought an outlet, first in a many-channelled river, emerging at Degerfors, Närke, in Sweden, and later, as the land near Denmark sank, through

Fig. 4

Fig. 4   The Ancylus Sea (about 6800–5800 BC). The Baltic was now a freshwater lake flowing out through central Sweden. Large parts of Finland were still under water, but the land began to be outlined. After Matti Sauramo

the present Belts. When the water-level in the Ancylus sea had sunk to that of the ocean, salt water entered via Danish sounds, and the Baltic, through the intermediate stages of the Mastoglo-gloia sea and Litorina sea, gradually assumed its present form. During the Ancylus period Finland was still a relatively narrow peninsula, growing westwards and southwards. Many impor-tant changes took place during the long Litorina period, the large fresh-water lakes Päijänne and Saimaa acquired outlets to the south, and Lake Ladoga a new exit to the Gulf of Finland through Neva. The land rose most rapidly in the north – even at the present day Ostrobothnia by the Gulf of Bothnia is rising 100 cm. each century, compared with 50 cm. in the region of Turku and only 30–40 cm. near Helsinki.

Fig. 5

During the long period in which the land was being formed, there were naturally great changes in the climate and in conse-quence in the flora and fauna. The chronological table makes comparisons between prehistoric periods and changes in nature such as afforestation, climatic change, and development of the Baltic. Immediately after the melting of the ice, the climate of Finland was cold and arctic, a tundra of grass and low scrub the only vegetation. With the gradual improvement of the climate in the pre-boreal period came the forests, mainly of birch at first, as is still the case on the margin of the forestarea in Lapland. Next came pine, becoming during the boreal period as common as birch, and occasionally more common, as the continental climate with dry and warm summers and cold winters was very favourable to it. Hazel and elm appeared, and during the fol-lowing warm and damp Atlantic period deciduous trees domi-nated, birch, alder, lime and oak being found as well as hazel and elm. The hardwood trees are found as far north as Oulujoki, and *trapa natans,* till now confined to Central Europe, reached up to central Finland. Towards the end of the Atlantic period, however, deciduous trees died out and spruce grew commoner, a development which has continued up to the present. Most Finnish Stone Age cultures belong to the climatically favourable Atlantic period, the Litorina stage of the Baltic, but the earliest traces of mankind come from the preceding epoch, the boreal and perhaps also the pre-boreal period.

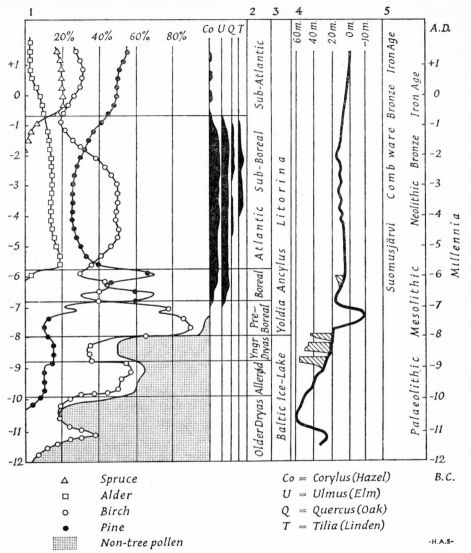

Fig. 5 *Diagram showing conditions in Finland in the late Quaternary. 1 Vegetational development; 2 climatic periods; 3 Baltic phases; 4 shore-line displacements of the Baltic for the 15 m. Litorina isobase (hatched areas signify the lake stages); 5 the prehistoric periods (absolute chronology by the varved clay method). After Matti Sauramo*

CHAPTER II

The Mesolithic Period

THE OLDEST DWELLING-SITES of the Stone Age in Finland are near Porvoo, some miles east of Helsinki, in the parish of Askola, whence it is usually named Askola culture. There are six sites, and all the material is uniform; organic material such as bone and horn has not survived, nor have fireplaces or structures been found. The artifacts are almost all made of a shiny smooth quartz, which may be a translucent pink or even rock crystal. The raw material was evidently derived from a local quarry, in a low hill called Kopinkallio with narrow (up to one metre wide) veins of quartz which had been cut out. On the level sand at the foot of the face were found loose pieces of quartz, including some worked in the same way as those from other sites at Askola, good evidence that the quarry belongs to that culture.

Axes are almost entirely absent, chisels more common. Scrapers and burins, arrowheads, rasps, augers and other tools with sharp points are characteristic. Among the coarse objects of uncertain form a number of excellent and very skilfully finished examples occur, whose closest parallels are to be found in the flint industry of the early Stone Age in central Europe, particularly round Hamburg, and closer at hand in the Komsa culture of the Arctic coast. The Komsa culture is characterized by coarsely-made objects of very hard stones such as hornblende, quartzite, greenstone, and dolomite flint. Flint-bearing strata are not found in Finland, so flint was replaced by quartz, making comparison between forms of objects from Askola and central Europe difficult. The resemblances are nevertheless such as to suggest that reindeer hunters from the latter region, following the retreating ice edge northwards in pursuit of game brought the technique with them. They must have followed the coast eastwards to Ladoga and then westwards again along a spit running out into the Yoldia sea to Askola.

The resemblances between Askola and Komsa objects are obvious, and it has been suggested that they are derived from a common source, and that the Komsa people continued north along an ice-free route which even at this early date existed between the White Sea and the inland ice, whilst the Askola people turned west. The relatively mild climate of the arctic coast at this time made permanent settlement possible, and the sea afforded catches of fish, seal and fowl. This interpretation is not the only possible one. Some consider that the Komsa culture is derived from the east European plain, perhaps even from Siberia, others that the Komsa people originated in an interglacial period and survived on the Norwegian coast. A third view is that a tribe moved north from Hamburg, and reached the White Sea along the west coast of Norway.

Its resemblance to the Komsa culture enables us to date the Askola culture to the pre-boreal period, 8,000 BC, and this is confirmed by comparison of the Stone Age sites in the Porvoo river valley. Here a continuous series of dwelling sites of the subsequent Suomusjärvi culture, is found, distinguished by its artifacts from the more archaic Askola. The sites lie lower than the Askola ones, and are therefore later; as the Suomusjärvi culture has been held on geological grounds to extend from the seventh to the fourth millennium BC, the Askola culture is to be allotted to the eighth.

The Askola culture was only discovered during the last ten years and our knowledge of it is still in many respects sketchy. As yet only one other site is known from elsewhere in Finland, and that is from a much later time than the ones at Askola itself, so that one cannot yet estimate the importance of this culture for the country as a whole until more finds are available.

The axe appears only in the later stages of Askola, when other stones as well as quartz came into use as raw material. It is one

Fig. 6

of the main forms of the Suomusjärvi culture, which is named after the parish in south-west Finland (south Finland proper) where its first sites were found. As the map shows, Finland proper and Uusimaa constitute the main area of its distribution, but sites belonging to it are scattered along the whole of the north coast of the Gulf of Finland as far as Karelia. In Ostrobothnia they form a continuous belt along what was then the sea coast, and is now, as the land has risen, quite high up the rivers, some 100 metres above sea level. In the interior this culture appears only sporadically.

Fig. 7

The Suomusjärvi people did not make pottery, and their culture is therefore sometimes also called 'preceramic'. The culture's main type is a coarsely formed, very roughly ground, stone axe, of oval section and with sharp corners. Chisels are also important, among them some carefully ground with sockets and round backs, large broad-bladed slate spears, and hemispherical club-heads with conical shaft-holes. The clubheads are often decorated with incised lines. Among the quartz objects are found scrapers and burins and small arrowheads with transverse or oblique edges, showing that the bow was known. Grindstones and hones are also found. Typical of the older sites is the random use of different stones as raw material; diabas, diorite, hornblende slate, uralitic porphyrite and others were used, so that it seems that people did not at first know of the excellent stone which the country possessed. During the long period the culture covered there were changes, and old types were replaced by new. Stone of better and better quality was used, until in the last stages the superb schist from north Finland is dominant.

Suomusjärvi dwelling sites lay mainly on the coast. Like most Stone Age sites they scarcely show on the surface, and are usually discovered purely by chance. The characteristic form is a culture layer lying beneath the tilth and upper soils, and containing charcoal, ashes, soil reddened by fire, bits of bone, quartz, broken stone objects, etc. Pottery does not occur until the ensuing period.

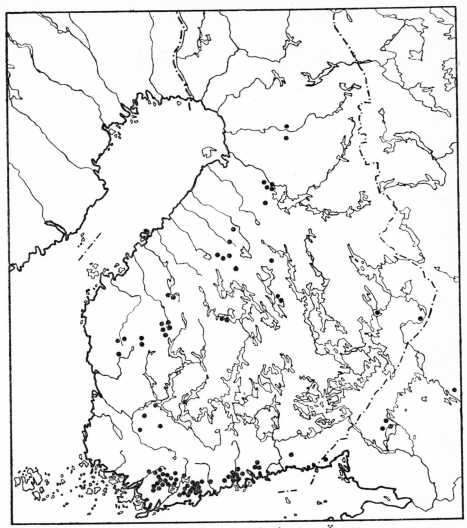

Fig. 6   Distribution of Suomusjärvi culture sites in Finland. After Aarne Äyräpää

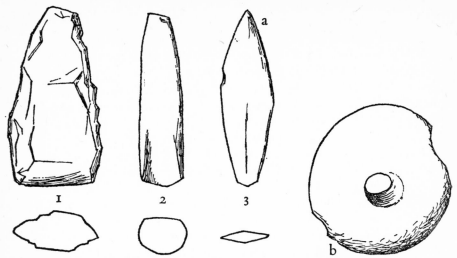

Fig. 7   a. Typical objects of the Suomusjärvi culture. 1 Axe and 2 gouge, found in Suomusjärvi; 3 spearhead of slate from Punkalaidun. Lengths 15.5, 15, 15.5 cm. b. Perforated stone disc. Suomusjärvi. Max. diameter 13 cm.

Fireplaces of stone are common, and remains of one dwelling have been found: the bottom of an oval hut with square porch.

The different heights above present sea-level of remains from various periods are fundamental for Stone Age chronology, as the whole dating is based upon it. The oldest Suomusjärvi sites lay on the coast, but as the land rose and the sea retreated, the settlers were compelled to move their dwelling sites to stay in contact with the sea. Thus the earlier sites are further inland and higher than the later, and this is true not only of Suomusjärvi but of the whole Finnish Stone Age. The scale of distance varies, depending on the rate at which the land rose, but it has been possible to establish a general relative chronology. The absolute chronology on the other hand must be based on geological cri-teria. In Suomusjärvi itself the oldest sites are 60–70 metres above sea level, which would date them to 6000–5500 BC, and in the Askola district they seem to be 500 years earlier. It may seem that a thousand years here or there is not very important in considering a past so distant, but the question of the date of Suomusjärvi culture is closely connected with its origins.

South of the Gulf of Finland flourished a Mesolithic culture, named after Kunda near the north coast of Estonia. It forms an eastern parallel to the western Maglemose culture in Denmark and it, too, was a fishing culture, using bone as the main material for tools. The Kunda people seem to have come from east central Europe, from Poland and the region round the Dnieper. The Suomusjärvi people in Finland are believed to be derived from the Kunda people and the Vöisiku people who succeeded them. Comparison of the two cultures is hindered by the absence from Suomusjärvi sites of the bone articles so characteristic of the Kunda culture, but resemblances in stone articles, weapons and tools, suggest that the forms came to Finland from the south. The view that the population was newly arrived from the south is strengthened by the great variety of stone used, which suggests immigrants at first unaware of the country's natural resources. The new settlers arrived by two routes, by sea to south-west Finland, and by land along the Karelian isthmus. The well-known find from Antrea may be connected with immigration along the eastern route; the oldest finds in the south-west have been associated with entry by sea.

The find from Antrea in Karelia consists of the remains of a net of willow bast with floats of bark and stone sinkers, and a number of whole and fragmentary objects of bone, horn, and stone. They were found in a marsh on the clay 90 cm. below the surface, having probably been lost in a channel between Ladoga and the Baltic, perhaps when a fisherman's boat sank with all his gear. The man himself must have escaped – there are no human bones in the find. What was then the lake bed is now marshy pasture, and mud and peat have built up over the clay. The bone objects are made of elk and swan bone, and include flat and socketed chisels, an awl, and significantly a spear point

Plate 1
Figs. 8, 9

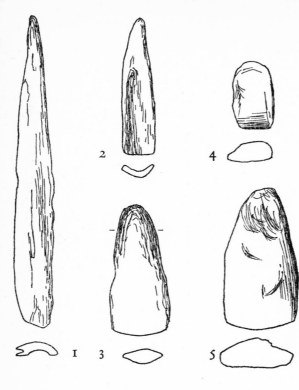

Fig. 8 Objects from the Antrea marsh find, Karelia. 1, 2 spearhead and gouge of bone; 3 axe with a rounded edge, made of elk antler; 4, 5 axe and chisel of stone. Length of spearhead 27 cm.

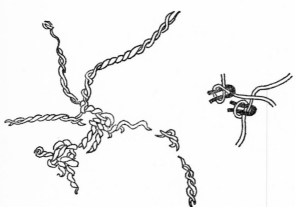

Fig. 9 Remains of net from the Antrea marsh find

26

or knife with a deep groove in one edge. According to its discoverer small microliths of quartz were embedded in this groove when it was found, and another similar object from the find has been lost. The find also includes a horn axe, some stone axes and chisels, burins, etc. Spearheads edged with microliths (of flint) occur in both the Maglemose and Kunda cultures. The find as a whole resembles the latter more closely, and an eastern connection is shown by the two fragmentary objects of Onega green slate, a type of stone which was imported into Finland all through the Stone Age, from the region north of Petroza-vodsk on the west side of Lake Onega, where it is found *in situ*.

The Antrea find has been dated to the transition between pre-boreal and boreal periods, the eighth millennium BC. Other iso-lated finds can be given approximately the same date; a toboggan or sledge-runner from Heinola, an ice-pick from Kirkkonummi, west of Helsinki. Whilst the ice-pick has parallels in the Kunda culture the sledge-runner is unparalleled in both Maglemose and Kunda. Sledge-runners of the Stone Age are found only in a region running from the Urals to Finland, and it is possible that the Heinola find represents an even more eastern element than the Kunda culture, though in the absence of comparative ma-terial it cannot be allotted to any particular culture.

Fig. 10 Spearhead of bone, tipped with flint microliths. Maglemose culture

To return to the question of the origins of the Suomusjärvi culture, it is true that it has certain forms in common with the Askola culture. Some of the burins, scrapers, oblique and trans-verse edged arrowheads have no parallels in Kunda, and for this reason some have seen the Askola culture as a forerunner of Suo-musjärvi, which would imply a wholly Finnish internal devel-opment, further supported by the absence from both Kunda and Vöisiku cultures of the broad-bladed slate spearheads, clubheads with conical shaft-holes and other objects characteristic of Suo-musjärvi. A decisive answer to this question will depend on the eventual dating of Suomusjärvi and evidence of the extent of the Askola culture in space and time. A possible internal develop-

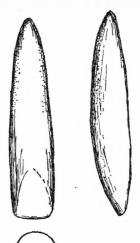

Fig. 11   Axe of the Ilomantsi type, Karelia. Length 23.7 cm.

ment does not necessarily exclude the arrival of new settlers, for the period is one in which large parts of northern Europe were inhabited for the first time, and the populations might easily have consisted of very various elements. As yet, however, we only have predecessors for the Suomusjärvi culture in the Askola culture's area.

There are traces of people other than those representing the Suomusjärvi culture at this period, outside their area, and particularly in the east of Finland, where more Stone Age sites with primitive stone axes have been found. One of these types, the Ilomantsi axe, a transverse edged axe of segmental cross section, is characteristically Karelian. The type is common in Olonets, and the material is usually the Onega green slate mentioned above. Eastern Finland was clearly in close contact with the Onega region, and it is probable that there was some immigration thence to Finland, bringing the new axe-types.

When we remember that the Suomusjärvi culture lasted 3000 years it is natural that it should have passed through many phases

Fig. 11

in which different stages can be defined. But in all these changes it retained its character as a hunting culture, with fishing, hunting and sealing as its resources, which required a half-nomadic existence, a yearly circulation round those places with the best catches. This mobility, determined by economic factors, is a constant feature of the Finnish Stone Age to its very end; the culture remained the same though its weapons and implements were improved and altered. The variation in finds does not imply any fundamental change in existence, but has other causes. Whether these are influences, immigrations or other factors is often very difficult to establish just because one is dealing with a very mobile population. And there is scarcely any anthropological material from Finland's Stone Age, which increases the problems of investigating the antecedents of the Suomusjärvi people and their successors.

Chapter III

The Neolithic Period

THE COMBED-WARE CULTURE

Fig. 12

WHILST WE HAVE no pottery from the Suomusjärvi people, who had not yet learnt or invented the potters' craft, their Neolithic successors provide us with an important clue to their dating and relative chronology by their different styles of pottery. The succeeding culture takes its name from the decoration on its clay vessels, which is reminiscent of the impression made by a comb, but more probably produced by a toothed stamp rather than a comb. Variations on this ornament, applied to the same large vessel with pointed or rounded bottom, were widespread over a great part of eastern Europe, where conditions of daily work and life seem to have been identical. This uniform area constitutes the combed-ware region which included, as well as Finland, the eastern Baltic area, East Prussia and north Russia. Its western border runs from Finnmark to the Gulf of Bothnia, and west of the Åland islands to the mouth of the Vistula, crosses the river Vistula in some places and then turns east, to follow the southern edge of the forest region across Russia up to and beyond the Urals. Naturally a pottery type so widely distributed shows local variations, and modern research has distinguished at least three combed-ware regions: the Baltic area, the Volga-Oka region, and the Urals. Finland and the east Baltic belong to the first, but show influences from the second.

The whole combed-ware region was based upon a hunting economy, fishing, hunting and gathering berries and edible plants, as well as seal hunting on the coast. Agriculture and stock farming were unknown, and the only domestic animal was the dog.

The chronological stages of Finnish combed ware are derived both from its ornament and its fabric; the shape of the vessel on

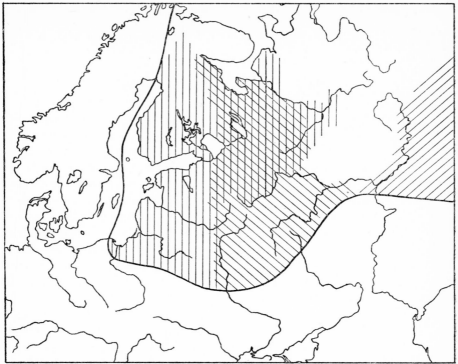

Fig. 12   Extension of the combed-ware culture in Europe. Hatched areas denote (from l. to r.) Baltic, Volga-Oka, and Ural regional types.

the whole remained unaltered, the usual type being the large vessel with pointed or rounded bottom, though small bowls also occur. A consistent feature is that the whole exterior of the vessel is ornamented; but the style of ornament changes, and this change can be equated with the land's rising, so that pottery in the highest (and earliest) finds is differently decorated from that in the lower (and later) ones. Early combed ware runs from 3000 to 2300 BC, the middle or typical period from 2300 to 2000 BC and the later from 2000 to 1800 BC. Within each of these groups an earlier and later form can be distinguished, as well as one or two local groups. The latest type of all, the comparatively little known Pyheensilta pottery (1800–1600 BC) was discovered only recently. It is these four types of pottery which allow us to follow the continuing changes in the extent of habitation and cultural connections during the period. Stone objects changed so little within it that they alone cannot give enough help to date dwelling sites and other remains.

Whence the potters' craft came to Finland, and how it spread is not yet established, but there is no question of indigenous invention. It is possible that it was introduced from the south, from the area round the Dnieper in the western Ukraine, where there are some resemblances to the early combed ware of Finland. Some stone objects also show certain resemblances, particularly the 'cradle-rocker' axes which can be compared with the shoe-last axes of the Danubian I culture, and the small clay idols which may be indirectly derived from the Ukraine. On the other hand the earliest combed ware has so many motifs in common with the south Scandinavian so-called 'megalith pottery' that this cannot be coincidental but demands some common origin, and some early combed-ware pottery has features which undoubtedly point to connections eastwards with the Urals. There is no single predecessor known to us from which the earliest Finnish pottery can be derived, and the problem is complicated by the fact that the particular style in question is not known in the eastern Baltic, but does occur on some east Karelian sites and even further east. The decoration is so individual that one is tempted to regard it as a native product, though of course under foreign influences. The technique itself, the manufacture of pottery must certainly have come from abroad.

It is clear that the combed-ware culture of Finland is a direct continuation of Suomusjärvi, a further development in the direction of greater richness and variety. Its stone and quartz forms are derived from its predecessor, and primitive axes of Suomusjärvi type have been found on early combed-ware sites. The area

Fig. 13

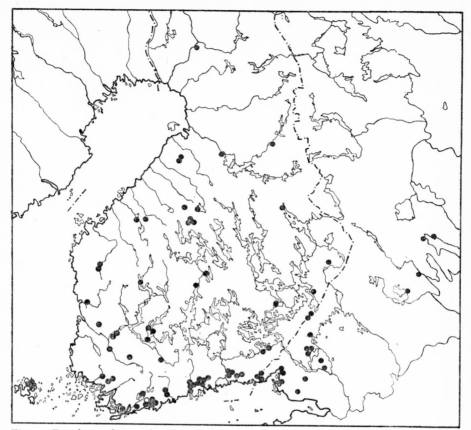

Fig. 13   Distribution of sites with early combed-ware pottery in Finland. After V. Luho

of settlement also shows a continuity; the early combed-ware sites were, like those of Suomusjärvi, in general on the coast. The most northerly combed-ware site is near the Arctic circle in Rovaniemi.

The more widely distributed middle combed ware occurs over most of Finland, the most northerly point again being Ro-vaniemi. The richest finds are from the Karelian isthmus and

Fig. 14

33

Plate 2

the region round Ladoga, and it appears that the style spread from there partly north-westwards to the lake district of the interior, partly along the north coast of the Gulf of Finland to south-west Finland and Åland. The best and most beautiful vessels in the style come from sites on the lakes in Savo, such as those from Pääskylahti in Sääminki, which are magnificent specimens of their kind.

It seems that this middle typical style developed in the Ladoga district, but it is difficult to say whether its extension westwards is a matter of immigration or cultural influence. If one considers how difficult these clay vessels were to transport, and how unsuitable as trade objects, it seems most likely that they were made at the places where they are found, and that it was the technique and decoration which spread, perhaps through the agency of emigrant groups. We know that the Stone Age people lived a very mobile life.

But it is also possible, as has been suggested, that the typical combed ware came to Finland with new immigrants from Russia whose main route lay through the Ladoga district. This view is supported by finds of Russian flint (probably from the Valdai district) which have been made on the sites of this type in Finland.

Plate 3

Another is the east European pitted ware which appears at the end of the period in Karelia, at Ladoga, and the Karelian isthmus. This pottery, whose ornament is almost exclusively formed of round or rhomboid depressions, with very little comb ornament, is typical of the Oka river basin and the upper Volga, and apparently spread into Finland from the south-east, over the Onega-Ladoga region. Fragments of this ware have been found as far west as the Kymi river and as far north as the Oulu river.

The two last phases of the style, late combed ware and Pyheen-silta, are mainly restricted to south-west Finland where they evidently originated. Finds of the former have been made also south of the Gulf of Finland, and it is clear that there were sea-

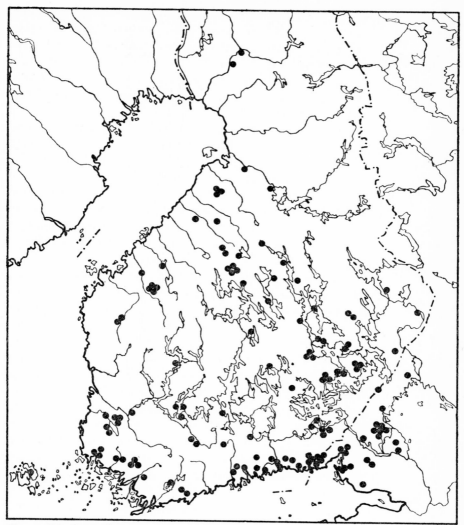

Fig. 14   Distribution of sites with typical combed-ware pottery in Finland. After V. Luho

borne contacts between Finland and the east Baltic lands, Pyheensilta pottery often has features, such as the marked neck of the profile, showing influence from east Swedish pitted ware. This latter only occurs in Finland in the Åland islands, and this Swedish influence was presumably transmitted to Finland via the islands. Only in isolated cases has Pyheensilta pottery been found outside the west coast district.

Plate 4

As has been said, the combed-ware people lived on what they caught, mainly fish, and it was because of fishing that they usually chose dwelling sites on sandy southern slopes by the water. Postholes show that the dwelling was usually a conical tent of poles with a diameter varying from 2–3 metres to 5–6.

Fig. 15

The reconstruction drawing of a hut whose remains were found at Pitkäjärvi in Räisälä parish in Karelia is often referred to and reproduced. The skeleton of this building was formed of a ring of poles which evidently supported a horizontal frame against which other poles were leant to form sloping walls. The frame was covered with skins, bark, brushwood or turf. The house had a square porch.

Round the hut there was sometimes a stone circle, and the floor inside this was somewhat lower. In the middle of the hut there would usually be a round fireplace, evidently to warm the room which was used only for sleeping. During the day people lived outside, at least in summer, and this must have been pleasant enough in the mild and favourable Atlantic and sub-boreal climate of Finland at this time. This way of life is illustrated by the remains of a dwelling site at Säkkijärvi near Viipuri where, outside a hut which could hold fifteen people, a whole family group, no less than three cooking hearths with remnants of meals in each were found. The hearth inside the hut on the other hand showed no signs of cooking.

The hut of poles was used throughout the whole Stone Age, but it was not the only form of dwelling. At some early combed-ware sites traces have been found of dwellings partly or

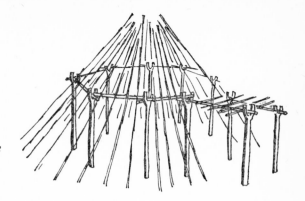

Fig. 15 Reconstruction of a Stone Age hut. After S. Pälsi

entirely dug down into the ground. These retained warmth better than draughty surface huts, and were more suitable as winter dwellings. Fireplaces were of stone, round or square in shape and about a metre across. Sunken fireplaces – pits filled with stones – were common, and some fireplaces quite devoid of stones are also found.

Plate 5

It is only during the last five or six years that graves certainly belonging to this period have been discovered in Finland. Patches of ochre including one or two objects of flint or amber, which could be interpreted as burials, had been known for a long time, but the first real graves were discovered as recently as 1959, and since then many more have come to light. All those as yet investigated are pits dug into the ground, and the burial in them is an unburnt body accompanied by red ochre. In the best-known grave field, that by Kolmhaara dwelling site, Honkilahti parish, south Satakunta, three different kinds of burial can be distinguished. Some were simple grave pits with no particular structural characteristics, other had upright stones at head or foot or both, and the third group consisted of cists built of red sandstone slabs placed on edge. In only a few graves were slight traces of the skeleton to be found, and in one it was that of a child ten or twelve years old. All the graves contained much red ochre; the simple graves had the richest grave goods, including a large

Plates 6, 9

number of beautiful and well-made flint objects, particularly arrowheads, and amber ornaments – in one grave no less than 60 amber beads.

It was a common practice in Neolithic cultures to cover the dead with red ochre. The nearest examples known are in east Karelia, Olenij Ostrov in Lake Onega, and further away in Russia, in the Vologda district and round the river Oka, and these are all regions from which many influences came to Finland. Ochre graves do not occur in the east Baltic lands but are found in East Prussia. There may perhaps be behind it some idea of preserving life in the grave – red is the colour of life.

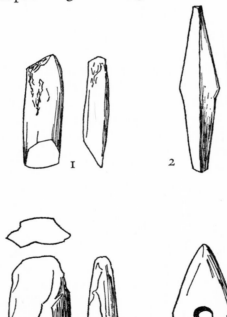

Fig. 16   Stone objects of combed-ware culture in Finland. 1 axe from Espoo; 2 spearhead from Laukaa; 3 axe from Pukkila; 4 rhomboid axe from Inkoo. Lengths 13.1, 11.1, 15.6, 24.4 cm.

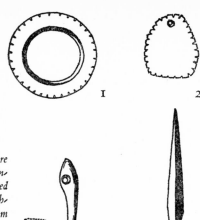

Fig. 17 Stone objects of combed-ware culture in Finland. 1 slate ring from Lapinjärvi, outside diameter 4.3 cm; 2 perforated slate ornament from Hämeenkyrö; 3 fish-hook from Viipuri; 4 arrowhead from Ilomantsi. Lengths 5.4, 4.2, 11.1 cm.

A common feature of the axes and chisels of the combed-ware culture is that they are usually transverse-edged (the axe is hafted so that the blade is at right angles to the shaft as in an adze) and well ground. Characteristic types are flat Ostrobothnian axes, 'cradle-rocker' adzes, the large Rovaniemi axes, four-sided axe and chisel types, curved back and other socketed gouges. Hunting gear is also common. Leaf-shaped spearheads are found at the beginning of the period, arrowheads become commoner, hook poles, fishing sinkers, net weights are also found. In spite of its richness, the material is very one-sided, almost everything of horn, wood, and bone having disappeared. And there are great differences in the surviving material as between different parts of Finland. Many types of stone object remained unchanged throughout the period but sometimes some chronological differences can be detected; for example, the curved gouge, the elliptical holed stone with pointed ends and the rhomboid form appear first in the late middle period. The same is true of imported goods – tools and material – as was pointed out above in describing Russian flint.

The combed-ware culture's stone tools and weapons are made of good material. The commonest is the fine schist which occurs

Figs. 16, 17

Plate 7

frequently in north Finland, whence came some of the objects in this material found in south Finland. A depot find of seven chisels of this sort of stone, from north Tavastia indicates the existence of a trade in them. Another natural raw material, above all in western Finland, was diabase, particularly Sata-kunta diabase which is found in sites south of Pori. Boat axes in particular (p. 48) were made of this sort of stone, and it seems that a local industry exported finished products.

The main imported raw material was Onega green slate, a fine-grained grey-green stone in which reddish veins can some-times be seen. It is very suitable for working and many of the most beautiful and best formed stone objects of Finland's Stone Age are made of it. The stone was exported from Olonets as half-finished or finished objects, and went to north Russia, Sweden, and the eastern Baltic region, as well as to western Finland. Such objects are so common in Karelia that they may be seen as rep-resenting a uniform culture covering east Karelia and Ladoga-Karelia. Finds from Antrea and Suomusjärvi show that the trade in green slate began in the Mesolithic period; it continued throughout the Stone Age.

Russian flint on the other hand seems to have been imported only during the middle combed-pottery period, and, unlike green slate, in the raw state. Piles of chips produced during flint working have been found on various dwelling sites. The most common products were small in size, such as arrowheads and scrapers, but some axes and spearheads are found. When the imports ceased at the end of the middle combed-ware period, local schist or quartz was substituted for flint.

A precious import brought from great distances was the amber used in ornaments found in all parts of Finland, even the extreme north. Most of these ornaments probably come from Samland in East Prussia, whence they were exported all over the combed-ware region. Only one Finnish amber ornament certainly derives from the other great European amber region, the west coast of

Jutland. It is a pendant in the form of a double axe, a type characteristic of the Scandinavian Passage Grave culture. The distribution of the finds suggests that the trade spread over the Karelian isthmus from East Prussia. One of the Karelian finds is a pendant with a man's face, found at Metsäpirtti on the west coast of Lake Ladoga. Though the amber trade was at its peak in the middle combed-ware period it lasted until the end of the Stone Age.

Plate 16

Flint was imported from Scandinavia as well as from Russia, particularly towards the end of the period, good examples being the hoard of four flint saws, and a dagger of white chalky flint. Other Scandinavian imports are polygonal shaft-hole axes, Swedish boat axes, T-shaped slate pendants, etc. Worthy of special mention are the objects of red, or red and grey striped slate found in northern Finland; daggers, knives, spear- and arrowheads. Some of the knives have handles shaped like animal heads; two elk, one bear, and one bird are known so far. The type of slate of which they are made occurs in north Finland, and their forms are common to the whole arctic region, so that it is not certain that they are imported. When the objects are of red slate from the mountains between Norway and Sweden their origin is unmistakable.

Objects of bone, horn and wood have only rarely survived, but two wooden harpoons were found together with the skeletons of seals which had died and sunk to the sea-bed before the hunter could recover them. Geological evidence suggests that this was seal hunting in the open sea (not on the coast) probably on the edge of the ice in early spring, as seals are still hunted in the Gulf of Bothnia today. One of the seals (from Närpiö) is Phoca Groenlandica, common in the Baltic during the Stone Age but disappearing later, probably exterminated by Stone Age hunters. The other seal (found near Oulu) is the common grey seal which still survives in the Gulf of Bothnia.

Other surviving organic materials are fish-hook barbs of bone, birch-bark holders for netsinkers of stone, wooden spoons and

Plate 8

some wood carvings. There are three spoons all with carved handles, one representing a bear, one an elk and one a bird. Two of them are carved in Cembra pine, which grows wild in north Russia and Siberia, with a western limit on the northern Dvina. The shape of the spoons is also eastern, and the closest parallels come from the peat bogs of the Urals.

The wide-ranging communications which these imports required depended on the transport represented by the finds of sledge-runners, some dozens of which, from different periods of the Stone Age are known from Finland. Their size suggests that they are from large strong sledges, so strong that they could undertake very long journeys, perhaps even as far as the Urals. It is possible that some enterprising merchants made very long journeys with dog teams, just as Arctic peoples do at the present day, but the possibility that the trade goods passed through many different hands from place to place cannot be excluded. The journey with a dog team from Finland to the Urals is an impressive one, but it is not impossible.

One boat alone, found in Helsinki, can certainly be ascribed to the Stone Age; this is a dug-out fir trunk, a light and seaworthy craft in whose construction fire was used to ease the work of hollowing out. It is geologically dated to 2000 BC, the end of the combed-ware period, but is not necessarily from that culture for it might just as well have belonged to the boat-axe people who at that time were beginning to immigrate into Finland. In the building of the Ladoga canal (in Russia), a fragment of a rough-bottomed oak dug-out was found which was dated to the combed-ware period. On the basis of this securely dated find one may perhaps allot to the Stone Age many of the hundreds of dug-outs found in Finland. The same argument might also be used of the skis, one of which has with certainty been dated to this period.

The main artistic product of the combed-ware culture is seen
in a number of animal-head sculptures in stone mainly from the

end of the Stone Age. They are either maces in the form of animal heads, or shaft-hole axes whose butt end is an animal head. Made in various types of stone, the best are of easily worked or green slate. The form varies, but there is no reason to make typological distinctions, and the individual artist's skill and imagination are the decisive factors. The most common type is an elk or bear, more or less naturalistically depicted. The very realistic elk head from Huittinen is a masterpiece, shaped with some artistic vision and great familiarity with the model, and the lively elk from Säkkijärvi also shows close observation and masterly execution. Although these implements are provided with shaft holes and shaped as axes, they are scarcely to be regarded as weapons in the ordinary sense of the word, intended for battle or the chase. They may have been borne on a chief's staff as symbols of authority, power and status, or they may have had something to do with magic cults. As it is Finland's largest wild animals, elk and bear, which are involved, they may hint at some cult connected with the chase, as well as showing how Stone Age people saw these animals, and how high the artistic standards of the best of them were.

Animal-head carvings have been found in widely separated parts of Finland, a pair, probably imported from the east, in Sweden and more in north Russia. One centre of production may have been in Russian Karelia – green slate from Olonets is often the raw material – but the carvings were also produced in Finland, as half-finished ones from Stone Age dwelling sites show local materials were sometimes used, as is also shown by the large elk head in wood from Rovaniemi which belongs to the same group.

Human heads are rare in Stone Age sculpture. One shaft-hole axe from Kiuruvesi in Savo has the base formed into a human head, but the treatment is not as naturalistic as the animal heads so that it is impossible to say whether it was intended to represent any particular model. A large, projecting nose is the most pro-

Plate 13

nounced feature, the eyes being merely indicated by depressions and mouth and beard not even hinted at, so that the impression of the whole is simply a broad and featureless face.

Plate 12

Other representations of men include a beautiful little sand-stone carving, one made of flint, and a wooden one from Poh-jankuru which has been said to represent a god. The face is crudely shaped, the nose straight and with a high bridge, the eyes marked by lines, the mouth clearly cut. This carving of fir wood has been compared with the geometrically ornamented wooden pillars from Gorbunovo in the Urals. They have a head cut at the upper end, and there is apparently some connection. The Finnish example is broken off under the shoulders, but has certainly been part of a large object as the head itself is 16 cm. high. Men are also depicted on one of the two rock paintings

Plate 14

found in Finland. They are both in the parish of Kirkkonum-mi some miles west of Helsinki. The one at Vitträsk contains geometrical figures mostly incomplete but well preserved. It is composed of a rectangle 40 cm. × 52 cm. with incised angular shapes and fringes on the sides and lower edge. The other, by Lake Juusjärvi includes at least eight figures, three hand prints, up to five fishes and a zigzag band perhaps representing a serpent, all coloured red.

The closest parallels come from arctic Norway, though some are found in Sweden, and there must be a certain connection, whether it be a similar hunting culture or some other explana-tion. The Finnish rock paintings belong in time either to the Suomusjärvi or to the combed-ware periods.

Plate 15

Whether these human figures are to be reckoned as pure art or given religious meaning is in general hard to say. In some instances a cult aspect seems almost certain, particularly in the so-called idols, small clay figures of men, sometimes in the shape of a phallus or an animal. Such 'idols' are known also from other regions of the combed-ware area, and have some resemblances to the south-east European idol group from whence the idea extended northwards from the Ukraine, whether by influence or actual migration. The south-east European element may have been a cultural borrowing of the late Palaeolithic, developed later under oriental influence.

In the usual terminology Neolithic or later Stone Age is used of a period with agriculture and animal husbandry by peasant farmers. In spite of contact with Scandinavia where agriculture and animal husbandry were introduced before the combed-ware culture reached Finland, they were not practised in Finland, or elsewhere in the combed-ware area. The allocation of this culture to the Neolithic period is justified by its achievements in other directions, particularly in pottery which was unknown to the earlier Mesolithic peoples. The highly developed stone-working techniques, far-reaching trade contacts and import of raw ma-terials all suggest a society far above a state of nature.

The nomadic life of these people explains why so many oc-casional dwelling sites have been found as well as the more permanent ones, and this factor was also likely to delay the estab-lishment of a settled society. People lived in small groups and families, and links between the groups were probably very slight. The large dwelling sites must have developed through people settling at the same place at perhaps widely varying intervals of time. But finds suggestive of some sort of village society are not entirely lacking. At a site at Kaukola in Karelia the houses seem to be grouped round a long narrow enclosure or main street.

The occurrence of combed-ware pottery as far north as Rova-niemi, near the Arctic Circle had already been mentioned. Dur-ing the last two decades one consequence of the new hydro-electric power stations and their controlled water supplies has been the discovery of many hundreds of Stone Age dwelling sites along the great rivers in Lapland. Many large dwelling sites have been investigated and a large number of objects recovered, though their publication remains a task for the future. The scantiness of pottery causes difficulties in dating, and the different stages are not nearly as clear in the north as they are in southern and western Finland. Many of the sites seem to have been in use over long periods, or at any rate in repeated use at widely separated times. Where combed ware occurs it naturally dates the site to that period, and other dating links are provided by imported objects such as the amber double-axe pendant (a type characteristic of the Scandinavian Passage Graves) or Swedish boat axes.

One characteristic of the end of the Stone Age in north Finland is the use of 'asbestos pottery'. Asbestos, a fine fibrous material, occurs as a binding medium in clay vessels from the earliest combed ware onwards, and its use continued throughout the Bronze Age and even into the Iron Age, but it is particularly frequent at this time, and widely spread, occurring not only in Finland but in northern Scandinavia and east Karelia, as well as occasionally further south. Its westernmost occurrence in Russia is in the region round Leningrad.

The Stone Age material from north Finland shows obvious resemblances to that of north Scandinavia and the Arctic Stone Age is often treated as a unity. The conditions of life and the natural milieu brought about resemblances in culture, and in the north the sea no longer separated Finland from Scandinavia. Combed-ware pottery extends over those regions in northern Europe where Finno-Ugric populations live or once lived. For this reason many have concluded that the combed-ware people were Finno-Ugrians. This is obviously possible, but one must remember that in so large a region groups which spoke different languages and different dialects must have existed. The community of culture does not contradict this, for cultures and languages are by no means always coterminous. No anthropological material is preserved and we cannot say to what race the people belonged. Some skulls from the period found in Estonia have been held to reflect two different racial elements, one of Europeans immigrating from the south, one of mongoloid type arriving from the east not later than the beginning of the period. Grave finds from the Ladoga canal in Russia point the same way, to a short, dolichocephalic population mixed with mongoloid elements from the east.

THE BOAT-AXE CULTURE

At the beginning of the second millennium BC, perhaps already by 2000 BC, a Stone Age culture appears in western Finland which has no roots in the combed-ware culture and clearly represents a new population. Characteristic forms are boat-shaped shaft-hole axes and comparatively small flat-bottomed clay vessels, often ornamented with cord impressions, which have given the culture its two names of boat-axe or corded-ware culture. It formed a part of the large European battle-axe culture complex, but in Finland as elsewhere independent local features developed. The complex covered a large part of Europe: Germany, Scandinavia, Poland, the eastern Baltic lands, Finland and some parts of Russia were all included. The origin of this culture is still disputed, some scholars seeking it in Saxony and Thuringia round the Elbe and Saale, others in southern Russia, perhaps round the lower course of the Dnieper. The boat-axe people were evidently nomadic or half-nomadic herdsmen who sought fresh pastures as the old were spoilt by drought or eaten bare. They arrived in Finland from Estonia, most likely by sea across the Gulf, as no trace of them has been found in Karelia and the isthmus. They probably arrived first in Uusimaa but quickly spread over western Finland, west of a line from the Kymi river through Tampere to Kokkola. East of this line no dwelling sites, and only sporadic isolated finds, of the boat-axe culture occur. This distribution in a clearly limited area indicates that we have to do with real immigration, not a new cultural influence. The region occupied is the most fertile, with the best climate and longest growing period. The dwellings lie

Fig. 18

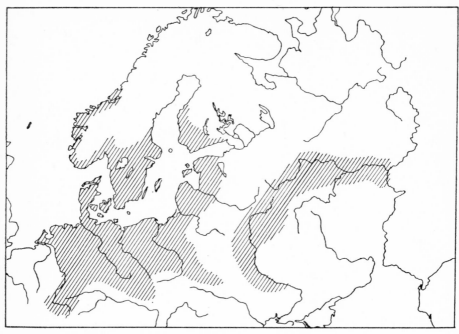

Fig. 18   Distribution of boat-axe cultures (corded-ware culture) in Europe

on sandy mounds and ridges near the clay soils which offered good pasture and rich soil, welcome to a race dependent on animal husbandry and perhaps also some agriculture.

Fig. 19

More than 800 boat axes have been found in Finland, but they may be divided into two main types, one common European, one a native Finnish form. The first clearly arrived with the immigrants and commonly has a rounded cross-section, straight profile and flat back, whilst the second has an angular cross-section, curved profile, a collar round the shaft-hole and a down-turned back with a hammer-like end. The raw material of the latter also strongly suggests native manufacture as 90% are made of olivine diabase, a stone which occurs only in lower Satakunta

Fig. 20

Plate 17

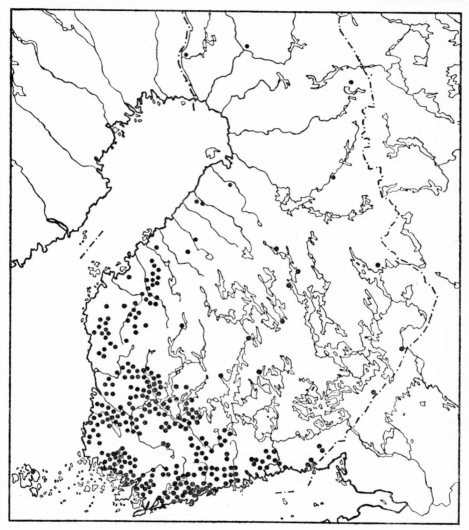

Fig. 19   Distribution of boat axes in Finland

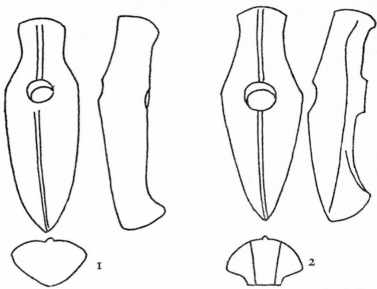

Fig. 20   Boat axes: 1 common European type; 2 Finnish type. Approx. length 16 cm.

in the region Pori – Rauma – Pyhäjärvi. It seems that an axe industry located here exported the native boat axe to the rest of the boat-axe culture region of Finland.

Plate 19

The pottery of this culture is distinguished from that of the combed-ware people by its flat bottom, S-shaped profile and smaller dimensions. Ornament (mainly the cord impressions mentioned above) is restricted to the upper part. On the bottom there is sometimes ray-ornament: similar decoration is found in the battle-axe cultures of the continent. The fabric of the pottery is harder than combed ware, and is mixed with sherds of burnt clay *(chamotte)*.

Among the characteristic tools of the boat-axe culture in Finland are axes with quadrilateral section and offset axes. It is noteworthy that no implements for hunting or fishing have been found in the house sites or graves of the culture, a great contrast to the combed-ware people which stresses how their way of life differed. Traces of houses are few, but they seem to have been dug into the earth. Graves usually lie in sand or gravel knolls, sometimes in the dwelling site itself. They are usually single, but are sometimes found in small groups; the dead were buried unburnt, in holes 0.5 to 1 m. deep, lying on one side with knees drawn up. The most usual grave furniture is a boat axe, a four-sided working axe and a clay pot, but the combination varies; sometimes there are two boat axes, and sometimes only pottery occurs. The graves are not marked on the surface and are found only accidentally.

Plate 18

The boat axe is a weapon, and the boat-axe people in Finland were conquerors, arriving at the end of the combed-ware period and settling among its people perhaps as an upper class. The original inhabitants continued to follow their original pursuits in hunting, perhaps retiring to the interior of the country, but contact between the two groups is suggested by features of their pottery; *chamotte* occurs in combed ware, and pits in corded ware. Animal-head sculptures are part of the combed-ware culture but they sometimes imitate boat axes, and from the frontier region between the two cultures come clumsy imitation boat axes generally made of poor soft stone, but only one genuine boat axe has been found in eastern Finland. On the other hand, communications thence to the east and south-east were evidently preserved, and some battle-axes of east European type reached the area.

It has been urged that the already established combed-ware people and the new arrivals could live in peace side by side, as they lived in different ways and there need not have been any economic conflict. But one must ask oneself whether the boat-axe people did not subjugate the original inhabitants. If they did, then they presumably took a share of the proceeds of their hunting. The absence of hunting gear from the boat-axe people's sites suggests they did not themselves hunt; but then it seems unlikely that where forest and lake offer such rich supplies of game and fish they were not content to restrict their diet to the produce of their own husbandry. Subsequent developments are another matter, for the new population had to adapt itself to the circumstances, adopt the country's old occupations, and merge with the original inhabitants.

The boat-axe culture in Finland was relatively brief, lasting only two or three centuries. Its absorption by the combed-ware culture produced Finland's last Stone Age culture, the Kiukais.

The expansion of the battle-axe cultures has been connected with the spread of the Indo-Europeans over Europe, and the time agrees well enough with the historical record of the arrival of the Hittites in Asia Minor at the beginning of the second millennium BC. The problem of the Indo-Europeans is mainly a philological one, but it has archaeological aspects. Numerous attempts have been made to equate archaeological cultures with Indo-European language groups. The most common view is that the centre of the expansion, the original home of the Indo-Europeans, lay somewhere between the Urals and Turkestan. It seems that the expansion of the Indo-Europeans across Europe was not the consequence of one great emigration, but was the result of repeated movements. Half-nomadic peoples moved at various times for various reasons so that the arrival of the first farmers in Denmark, the arrival of the battle-axe culture in Scandinavia, and the great extension of urn burial fields can all be seen as parts of the process. In other words, the battle-axe culture marks only *one* wave of Indo-European expansion. It has never been proved but equally never questioned, that the boat-axe people in Finland were Indo-Europeans. It has also been assumed that the appearance of this culture in the eastern Baltic indicates the arrival with it of the ancestors of the Letts and Lithuanians who settled there. In Finland on the other hand the culture is merely an interlude.

As mentioned above, the boat-axe culture in Finland is only an episode, a few hundred years, and not one which ever affected the whole country. The finds of its successor, the last Stone Age culture, come from the coastal district from Viipuri (Viborg) to south Ostrobothnia, and some have also been found in Åland. The axes from Kiukais sites are usually cross-edged like a adze, usually of segmental or rectangular cross-section, either tapering towards the back or parallel-sided. The chisel shapes are like the axes, only smaller and flatter. Shaft-hole axes also occur, some with pointed edge, and others with rounded head can be derived from boat-axe types, others are imported from Sweden or the east Baltic, or at least made under influence from these regions. Many of the animal-head carvings also belong to the Kiukais culture, and in its dwelling sites we find grindstones for the first time in Finland: they indicate that agriculture was practised, but they are accompanied by hunting gear, such as sinkers for fishing lines and nets, and arrowheads, showing that the Kiukais culture, unlike its predecessor the boat-axe culture, included the use of natural resources by both hunters and peasants simultaneously. Its pottery consists of flat-bottomed bowls which widen towards the top, of a coarse fabric including chalk pebbles. The main decorative motifs are round pits, horizontal furrows, and comb stamps. Textile impressions are also usual, and may be connected with the common expansion of 'textile pottery' in eastern Europe. This feature is shared by pottery from the interior of Finland in the southern and central regions and other features are shared by pottery from some dwelling sites on the Swedish coast in Gotland and Hälsingland.

The relative importance of the boat-axe and combed-ware cultures in the Kiukais blending of the two is largely a matter of individual interpretation. Some have stressed the obvious fact that the boat-axe people's agriculture and animal husbandry could not prosper in the ruling climate, and they were therefore compelled to adapt themselves to the sort of economy which all the Finnish Stone Age peoples had relied on. The loans from the combed-ware culture are thus seen as almost more important than those from the boat-axe culture, though the boat-axe people are seen as the decisive factor in the subsequent ethnic develop-ment. Others have denied any significant role to the boat-axe people, and see the Kiukais people simply as the sucessors of the west Finnish combed-ware people both culturally and ethnic-ally. These two contradictory views cannot be reconciled or judged as yet. But what must surely be allowed is that it is un-likely that all the boat-axe people died out or emigrated, and some therefore must have remained as one component in the later cultural ferment.

The connections of the Kiukais culture have been discussed above. The importing of amber and objects of both eastern and western flint continued. Finds show contact with the area south of the Baltic, with East Prussia and Estonia, but the closest con-nections were with the coastal districts of Sweden. This is par-ticularly clear in the case of the pottery, well shown by the finds from the Stora Förvar cave on Gotland. Investigations support the view that the Kiukais culture had a maritime character, and it is not unlikely that it will be seen in future as part of a unity embracing both sides of the Gulf of Bothnia.

THE STONE AGE IN ÅLAND

The Åland islands had a development of their own during the prehistoric period. Lying halfway between Finland and Sweden they were subject to influences from both. The oldest finds come from the north-east of the present main island, though most of it in the combed-ware period lay below sea-level and was under water. All the phases of the combed-ware culture are here repre-sented in an area of 2 or 3 square kilometres, the later finds always lower than the earlier. The early pottery was clearly brought by people from south-west Finland attracted by the opportunities for fishing and seal-hunting, and they evidently preserved good connections with the mainland as we see from their typical pottery and idols. Later pottery from the end of the Stone Age and the Bronze Age shows that the settlement was a continuing one.

At the end of the combed-ware period Åland received a new population from the west, from Sweden. The extent to which the land had risen made it possible now to use a larger area, which was settled by people of the Scandinavian pitted-ware culture. The best-known dwelling site is Jettböle in Jomala about 6 kilometres north of Mariehamn. During the Stone Age it lay on a small arm of the sea with good fishing and good shelter to the east and north-east. Two different zones can be distinguished most easily by their pottery. The later dwelling sites suggest by the presence of grindstones that some agriculture had been introduced.

A grave in which a skeleton survived was found in the dwelling site itself, and is probably to be allotted to the boat-axe culture: the body lay on its side with knees drawn up as was customary. The skeleton is the only one to survive from the Stone Age in Finland – it is the chalky soil of Åland that has preserved it – and the skull is of long narrow Nordic type. Unfortunately there were no grave goods.

Jettböle II, the later phase, has become particularly known for a multitude (fragments of at least 60) of human figurines of firm, fine clay. There is nothing corresponding to them in the Scandinavian pitted-ware culture, and possible influences have been sought in the combed-ware culture.

The development in Åland seems continuous throughout the Stone Age into the Bronze Age, but a change of population may have taken place when the pitted-ware culture arrived. In the oldest dwelling sites with this ware, however, late combed ware has also been found, and connections with mainland Finland seem never to have broken.

Plate 20

Plate 21

Chapter IV

The Bronze Age

FINLAND SHOWS in its first metal-using civilization, the Bronze Age, the same division into two regions found in the late Stone Age, where the Kiukais culture covered the western coastal regions and had strong connections with the areas west of the Gulf of Bothnia, and the asbestos pottery culture covered the inland regions. In the Bronze Age Finland was in contact with two great, flourishing culture regions whose influence was decisive. One was the Scandinavian, centred on Denmark and Skåne but extending over the rest of Scandinavia and north Germany, the other was the east Russian which stretched from the lower Kama to the mouth of the Oka, and in an eastward direction as far as the Urals, and was an important factor in all the regions north of its own area. The Scandinavian influence appears mainly in Finland's coastal region, the east Russian in eastern and northern Finland, though some Scandinavian bronzes have been found inland and even up in Lapland.

Plate 22

Fig. 21

The most characteristic remains in the western coastal districts are the grave mounds which lie in a scattered belt along the coast and island from the eastern to the western frontier, and are also numerous in Åland. These mounds, called in Finnish *hiiden-kiuas*, or 'giant's fireplace' are round cairns (only rarely rectangular or oval) built entirely of stones, and found usually on stony ground high above the water, remote from later Iron Age settlements. The size varies very much but a diameter of 10 to 15 metres is usual, though the largest are more than 30 metres across. They show no external structural features apart from an edging

Plate 21

Plate 24

of larger stones. Inside they sometimes have concentric rings of stones, sometimes a cist of flat stones on edge, sometimes dry stone walls of local stone. The cists are often as long as a man's body and one may conclude that they were used for

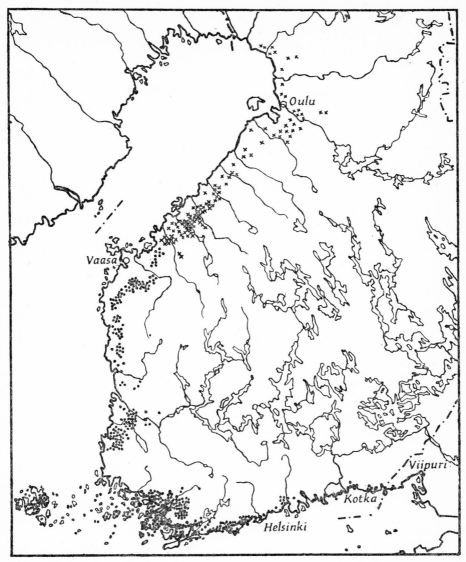

Fig. 21 Distribution of Bronze Age grave mounds in Finland. Dots denote sites that certainly, crosses those that probably, belong to the Bronze Age. After C. F. Meinander

inhumations, though no skeletal remains have been preserved. The few smaller box-like cists sometimes cover burnt bones, but cremation burials are usually found without any container. From Scandinavian parallels one would conclude that the graves with unburnt bodies belong to the earlier Bronze Age, and those with cremation to the later, but it is very rarely that any accompanying grave goods are found in the cairns so that it is not possible to draw any firm conclusions about their age.

A corresponding type of grave mound is found west of the Gulf of Bothnia and occurs there as far south as Skåne. In Denmark itself a large earth mound with a stone cairn inside is the dominating type in the early Bronze Age and is found as far north as Uppland in Sweden. The distinction is evidently produced by the availability of material. There are no precedents for these grave cairns in Finland, and it is clear that they come from the Scandinavian culture and spread north and north-east. Besides the cairns we find arrangements of stones in the form of a ship in Finland, though rarely. This too was originally a Scandinavian type, particularly characteristic of Gotland. The best-known and finest examples are from Åland, where they are found at Grytverksnäset as part of a whole complex including round mounds and level stone groupings. The 'ships' are oval, with edges made of large stones placed closely together, and interiors filled with stones to just below the height of the edge. Similar boat-shaped cairns are found in some places on the mainland of Finland, but it is not certain that they are from the Bronze Age, and they may be later. Some others have been found in the eastern Baltic lands, on Ösel and the west coast of the Gulf of Riga, and they have been regarded as evidences of influence from Gotland, and perhaps of colonization.

Only a few Bronze Age dwelling sites are known from the west coast of Finland, and the finds from them are almost entirely composed of a characteristic Bronze Age pottery. Traces of the dwellings are few, but indicate round houses; the houses are

Plate 23

Plate 25

better preserved in Åland, particularly Kökar, the remotest group in south-east Åland. The site is Otterböte where under high cliffs lie nine round hut floors, external fireplaces, refuse middens and the remains of a well. The foundations are stone circles like low walls, the floor in the middle slightly sunken, with a fireplace in the centre and round it some post-holes. A square porch is sometimes found in front of the door, and the huts were probably conical like the Stone Age hut at Pitkäjärvi, though they may have had vertical turf walls; the excavation provided no evidence.

The finds were almost entirely of pottery, 23,000 fragments from six of the hut floors, mainly of large barrel-shaped clay pots which were usually decorated with vertical lines drawn by fingers, though some were plain and some had textile ornament. The large number of seal-bones found is an important clue to the nature of the site, for the island was then much smaller than it is now, a mere rocky islet and the only reason men lived there was for the seal hunting. The huts probably reflect a seasonal settlement for the spring seal hunting, and the large clay tubs were to transport the oil. The hunters probably came from the west from Åland where the same sort of pottery, unknown on the Finnish mainland, is found.

Plate 27

All the northern countries depended on imports for their bronze, and the forms show that the metal came to Finland via Scandinavia. Their rarity shows that bronze was scarce and precious in Finland, and only 120 metal objects from the period have been found. The reasons for this may be various; the deposit of rich grave goods may have ceased to be usual, some graves may have been plundered and objects may have been recast, but the rarity of the finds remains striking.

Scandinavian forms are dominant in western Finland, and even the central European swords and other objects from far afield which are also found probably come via Scandinavia. From the early Bronze Age we find only weapons and tools; it is not until

later that ornaments and toilet articles appear. The weapons of
the earlier Bronze Age include splendid battle-axes, daggers
and palstaves, some swords, spearheads and one or two socketed
axes. Several later types of socketed axes occur also, among them
the Mälardal axe from central Sweden where there was a large
industrial production. Other late Bronze Age finds are swords
(including some fine ones from central Europe), spearheads,
'spectacle' brooches, ornamental pins, knives, tweezers and razors. The oldest gold object in Finland also dates from this period
and comes from a grave mound in Satakunta.

Plate 29

Few finds come from dwelling sites in western Finland, a
quarter are grave finds, the majority being chance finds. Two
hoards from Kokemäki should also be mentioned, one including
a spectacle brooch and a central European sword, the other mainly ornaments, two spectacle brooches, an ornamental pin, small
hammered bronze buckles (probably for a belt) and fragments
of a bronze cauldron. Even later is a marsh find from Eura in
Satakunta including three Scandinavian neckrings; it may be
immediately pre-Roman.

Plate 28

Most of these bronzes are clearly imported, and it seems likely
that finished products rather than the raw metal were introduced,
though some objects made in Finland have been found, including offset axes from the early Bronze Age and collared axes
from the later. They are unsuccessful castings which must have
been made locally, probably by recasting the metal of imported
goods.

Outside the coastal belt, in the eastern and northern regions
of the interior, the only fixed finds from the Bronze Age are
dwelling sites which had already been used in the Stone Age
and show that the same settlements continued into the Bronze
Age. Eastern influences were no novelty in this area, and the
rarity of bronze finds suggests that the metal was so little known
as to have made no significant alterations in the culture. It is
difficult and often even impossible to draw a line here between

Fig. 22 Bronze axe from Maaninka. Length 10.2 cm.

Stone and Bronze Ages, for the population, at least to begin with, continued at the Stone Age level. Niskanperä in Rovaniemi, a large dwelling site inhabited right through from the combed-ware culture's closing stages to the Bronze Age gives a good example of the continuity. On the other hand the finds of moulds from these dwelling places show that bronze-casting was known, and justify the use of the term Bronze Age. A native eastern axe type, the Maaninka axe, also shows that the culture had a certain independent identity, though the type developed under the influence of east Russian types. Some objects imported from east Russia are found, including from the early Bronze Age axes of the Seima type named from the grave field near Oka in Russia. Most of the east Russian bronze objects, like the moulds, are from the later Bronze Age and most of these are characteristic of its last phase, from 600 to 200 BC, the Ananjino culture named after a grave field on the lower Kama.

Fig. 22

The most important finds from the Finnish sites are of pottery, and from them the eastern Bronze Age in Finland can be divided into two sub-groups, an asbestos pottery and a textile pottery. The former covers mainly the area north of a line Tampere-Sortavala, the latter the area south of it, but both are difficult to date. The asbestos ware found in north Finland shows influence from

Russian pottery of the earlier Bronze Age, but asbestos ware is found all over the arctic region, in Norway, Sweden and the Kola peninsula. Textile pottery occurs in Finland already in the Kiukais culture and seems to have survived to the Iron Age, though most examples come from the last thousand years BC. Its use of pitting and combing as ornament connect it with central Russia, the region of the Oka and upper Volga, whence it spread slowly northwards. It is perhaps worth mentioning that in Russia it tends to be identified with Finno-Ugrian tribes.

The boundary between the areas using the two types of pottery in Finland is not rigid, and both are found on either side of the line. Metal objects evidently all come from the same region, the Urals, whence they were carried to north Russia, Finland and north Scandinavia; and there are other signs of contact between the different cultural regions of Finland. Textile ware has been found in the west coast region, as well as east Russian objects, and some Scandinavian bronzes have been found in eastern Finland. In the north two hoards point, one westwards to Scandinavia, the other eastwards to Russia.

Both these hoards belong to the later Bronze Age. The one from Sodankylä includes four Scandinavian bronze swords evidently hidden by a merchant from Norrland or north Norway. The other from Lusmasaari, an island in Lake Inari, included four twisted neckrings, three armrings, a knife and a socketed axe, all of bronze. Whilst the ornaments are of Scandinavian type the axe is a late variant of the Seima type, perhaps a local product. This hoard too might be a merchant's cache but one is inclined to believe that it belonged to a native, perhaps a rich 'Lapp'. In any case it shows cultural influences from two different directions.

The dwelling sites of both sub-groups are pure hunting lodges and nothing suggests that their inhabitants practised agriculture or husbandry, though these were known both in the Asva culture of Estonia and the gorodishche culture of the Volga-Oka region, which both belonged to the textile pottery area. The Finnish finds are particularly reminiscent of the Asva culture. The gorodishche people (named after their fortified dwellings sites) lived mainly by agriculture and animal husbandry and are generally supposed to have been Finnish tribes. The textile-ware people in Finland are assumed to derive from the combed-ware population and like them to be of Finno-Ugrian origin. Later they must have become Lapps or, insofar as they survived to the Iron Age, blended together with the Finnish tribes who arrived in the region about this time.

The people using asbestos ware have been identified as Lapps or rather, their predecessors. There are philological reasons for placing the immigration of the Lapps from north-east Russia into Finland and Scandinavia in the last millennium BC, and the eastern cultural influences mentioned above would thus be explained. A different explanation must be found for Finland's Scandinavian Bronze Age as the culture of the west coast is traditionally called. It has been supposed that the builders of the grave mounds on the coast and islands were strangers, seamen and merchants who settled in Finland, bringing with them their own burial customs and grave goods. It has been further supposed that there may well have been some hostility between them and the original inhabitants. On the other hand the maritime connections of the Kiukais culture with Scandinavia have been stressed, and it has been pointed out that it had every opportunity to develop into a metal-using culture. On this view, the inhabitants of the coast in the Bronze Age were mainly descendants of the Kiukais people, and the visible Scandinavian influences merely testify to good communications westwards. To clear up this problem one must compare conditions on the west coast of Finland at this period with those on the other side of the Gulf of Bothnia.

The cairn appears in both places as a new grave form and some claim that as the custom of burying the dead is above all characteristic of peasant farming cultures, the grave mounds on the coast of Norrland show the northward spread of farming and a farmer tribe, though there is no direct proof of this. On the other hand, the rich hunting places of inner Norrland with a population still in the Stone Age have been seen as the true source of the wealth of the new coast-dwellers, who taxed their primitive neighbours' harvest of fish, meat and hides, as a valuable source of income alongside their own agriculture. Shipping and trade formed a third factor, as through them links with the great central region in the south were forged.

We can well imagine that conditions in Finland were very similar, and with the arrival of Bronze Age civilization the coast-dwellers were in a key position. It was on the coast that the new culture was first implanted, and there it developed, at least in places, into the stable peasant culture of the later Bronze Age. Whether these coast-dwellers were new immigrants or an original native population is another question, but it is difficult to believe that the new burial customs and the new ideas which they reflect were only a cultural loan. It seems more likely that at least the first grave mounds were the work of newly-arrived Scandinavians who settled in Finland and whose customs were later adopted by the original population of the coast, and this is supported by the distribution of the bronzes. The oldest have been found mainly in the south of Finland proper round the town of Salo and it was perhaps here that the first Scandinavian immigrants settled, bringing their new burial customs and the use of metal. They may have enriched the Kiukais culture and helped its development into a true metal-using culture as we find it in its most developed form in the later Bronze Age in the lower reaches of the Kokemäki river in the parishes of Kiukainen, Nakkila and Harjavalta.

The new settlers, and perhaps the coastal population as well, linked western Finland in culture and trade to the Scandinavian areas. Contacts with the part of central Sweden around

Lake Mälar were particularly close as the Mälar axe and some ornaments typical of the region show, though they do not exclude the possibility of direct contacts with southern Scandinavia and the Continent, and the presence of some Continental merchants. The central European swords must in any case have come from Continental weaponsmiths. Gotland probably played a large part, as the ship-settings of stones suggest.

But the coast-dweller's contacts were not only overseas; they naturally profited from the products of the interior of Finland, furs, meat and fish, for it is difficult to see what apart from furs can have been bartered for the bronze.

The Scandinavian Bronze Age ended in its central area about 500 BC and iron slowly succeeded it. The decrease in finds suggests a general cultural decline, whether caused by a worsening of the climate, an interruption in trade, or only a new burial custom without grave goods. Scandinavian elements dry up in Finland and we cannot follow development beyond the middle of the millennium. It has sometimes been assumed that the Scandinavians were compelled to emigrate as the climate became too bad for agriculture and husbandry, but it is possible that by changing to a hunting economy they survived. As will be seen in the chapters on the Iron Age, the finds are too scarce to give any real idea of what happened.

CHAPTER V

The Iron Age in South-west Finland before AD 800

THE USUAL TITLE for the second half of the first-millennium BC, namely, the pre-Roman Iron Age, can only be used of Finland with some reservations. During this period there was no true Iron Age culture in Finland if we understand this to imply a society producing and using iron, and so the title is a misleading one. On the other hand to call it Bronze Age would be no more suitable, particularly as finds from the country's western Bronze Age cease at the beginning of this period, though those from the eastern Bronze Age culture continue somewhat longer, as objects belonging to the Ananyino culture show. Two of these come from the west coast, and as they belong to a time at which western bronze objects are no longer found, they have been interpreted as evidence that hunters from the east were extending their travels to districts which had been abandoned by the western Bronze Age population. But it has also been suggested that this population, as its supplies of bronze from the west dried up, began to obtain it from the east, though the rarity of bronze in eastern Finland makes this seem improbable.

Other finds from the period are scarce and heterogeneous. It appears that some at least of the textile pottery dwelling sites remained inhabited though in the absence of metal objects it is difficult to say for how long. A dwelling site near Porvoo in Uusimaa, with remains of the actual house, has been allotted to this period. Post-holes from a round clay hut and remains of a fireplace have been found, with fragments of Estonian Asva pottery, a grindstone, bits of iron slag and a piece of marsh-iron ore the size of a thumbnail. The slag was found in the tilth but the marsh-iron was in the find layer. The pottery comes from the last millennium BC.

Other fixed finds which in all probability belong to the period are some unimpressive grave mounds, generally low-lying, though the dating depends on their height above sea-level and the general character of their pottery as closely datable objects are wanting. From Åland there is a small grave find with a bronze pin which might come from the period, and the picture is completed by a sledge-runner and a ski found in marshes on the mainland, which have been geologically dated. Two bent iron swords or daggers found recently at Savukoski in Lapland probably belong to the Ananyino culture, and if this is so, open new vistas for the exploration of the period in north Finland.

This poverty of material, almost absolute in Finland, is also characteristic of the greater part of Sweden, where finds from 300 to 150 BC are very rare. Only in Gotland and Skåne is the gap closed, and even in Denmark the pre-Roman Iron Age seems poor compared with the richness in Bronze Age finds.

Some possible reasons have already been advanced. It has been suggested that some of the population emigrated because of changes in climate. Another view is that trade connections were broken by the expansion of the Celtic peoples in central Europe, compelling the inhabitants of the north, deprived of metal, to have recourse to native organic material which has not survived. The third view explains the absence of recognizable graves by a change in burial customs. The two latter views agree in holding that the decline is apparent only, an absence of evidence rather than of population.

None of these views seems satisfactorily applicable to Finland. The change in climate was scarcely as devastating as used to be assumed; at its peak it might have induced some farmers to seek more favourable conditions elsewhere, but it is unlikely to have affected the hunters at all. The gradual cessation of trade must have affected farmer and hunter alike, but it must be remembered that the eastern and western Bronze Age peoples in Finland were parts of two quite differently orientated cultures, and any drying-up of western metal supplies would have affected only the coastal districts. Similarly a change of religion, if one can consider the matter in such terms at this period, is quite unlikely to have af, fected both peoples simultaneously.

The problem is at present insoluble, though the absence of finds is not evidence that Finland was uninhabited in this period. We cannot however speak of a continuous development in sites or culture from the Bronze Age to the true Iron Age as occur, red in the first centuries of our era, nor can we point to a single dwelling site or burial ground used through this period of five centuries. The finds suffice only to show that the country was inhabited, but not to bridge the gap from the Bronze Age to the true Iron Age.

Fig. 23   Distribution of cemeteries of the early Roman period, first two centuries AD

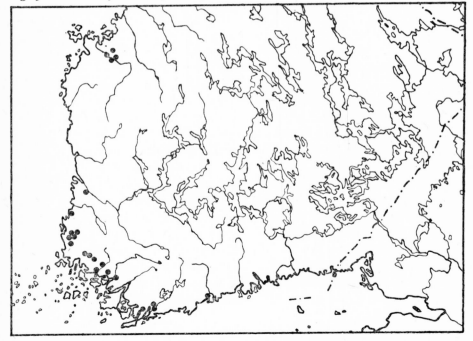

The Iron Age in Finland began as recently as the first centuries of our era, and lasted much longer than in western or central Europe, for it is only in the twelfth century that written sources became available for western Finland. In the intervening thousand years and more, large parts of Finland were uninhabited waste, and at least four separate Iron Age groups can be distinguished: south-west Finland, southern Ostrobothnia, Åland and Karelia. They were separated by large expanses of deserted territory, and their metal-using began at different periods and continued for varying lengths of time so that it seems more natural to treat them separately, mentioning their influence one on another as appropriate.

The most important of the four is that in south Finland which developed into the heartland of the Iron Age cultures of Finland, and hence we deal first with it, distinguishing for convenience a local early Iron Age from a later.

THE EARLY ROMAN PERIOD (AD 1-200)

In the first centuries of our era, beginning about AD 50, cemeteries were established on the south-west coast of Finland whose many weapons and tools are of iron. The cemeteries are mainly near river mouths extending from Karjaa in western Uusimaa to the neighbourhood of Uusikaupunki, 60 kilometres north of Turku. In addition a single large grave field is known from Penttala in Nakkila at the mouth of the Kokemäki river. These cemeteries usually lie near modern settlements often on southward-facing slopes cultivated at the present day, and later Iron Age burials also follow this siting which differs from the Bronze Age one, as does their structure.

Some of these large cemeteries (Kroggårdsmalmen in Karjaa, Koskenhaka in Piikkiö, Penttala in Nakkila) are paralleled in Estonia and northern Latvia, and are called by an Estonian term *tarand* cemeteries. The characteristic feature is a stone structure, a

Fig. 23

Fig. 24

Plate 30

long stone-edged enclosure divided into small rectangular chambers and cells. The cemetery is usually aligned along a ridge on the brow of a hill so that the cells lie athwart the length of the ridge. The kernel of the whole is one cell, and in course of time, new cells were constructed along each of its long sides so that a long narrow grave field developed. The earliest of these chambers were used for inhumation burials, but later the bodies were first cremated; the cell was then covered with stones so that eventually a long continuous cairn took shape.

Estonian *tarand* graves are widely distributed and were in use for many centuries as new cells were added to the earlier ones. They represent large and stable peasant communities, which according to Estonian scholars had a continuous development from the Bronze Age; the *tarand* is held to be developed from the Bronze Age and pre-Roman Iron Age grave-cairn with a stone cist. In Finland the *tarands* are a new type of grave and often only *one* cell is found, so that it seems more likely to have been introduced by immigrants from the southern coast of the Gulf of Finland.

All the *tarand* graves in Finland belong to the Roman Iron Age (AD 1–400), the largest being from the first and second centuries which are also represented by other grave forms. There are some cemeteries with individual burials, quite unlike the collective burials of the eastern Baltic. The best known and most important of these is Kärsämäki on the outskirts of Turku. Here the occupation layer of a scattered Stone Age dwelling site had been broken into by many graves of the Roman period. Almost all were cremation burials (only three inhumations were recorded as opposed to seventy cremations) covered with stones. The burnt bones and grave goods were placed on one flat stone and then covered with others, but there were also some urn burials where the bones were deposited in a clay or wooden vessel, and others in which the bones were simply gathered in a pile without any protection. The inhumation burials were covered by an exten-

Plate 31

Fig. 24 Plan of a tarand *grave field. Kroggårdsmalmen, Karjaa, Uusimaa*

ded pattern of stones. These burials are quite foreign to the eastern Baltic, but have parallels in Sweden and in the so-called 'Gothic' culture of the lower Vistula. Whether the burials are derived from Sweden or represent colonists from the Vistula is as yet undecided, but the finds make the latter alternative seem more likely.

Some round cairns in Laitila in northern Finland proper deserve special mention. Beneath them were found graves dug into the ground containing burnt bones and the remains of the pyre. In one or two cases the grave was big enough to have held an unburnt body but did not contain any bones. A grave pit under a cairn is not a Finnish burial form, and nor is it known from the eastern Baltic. Corresponding burials are known from Sweden, particularly Gotland, where both inhumation and cremation burials from this period have been found beneath stone cairns, often in a grave pit.

Some other cairns without special structural features may also belong to this period. The cairn remained characteristic of Finnish burial customs during the whole of the Iron Age and in a country as stony as Finland this seems natural enough.

The material from finds of the first two centuries is all of foreign origin, and resembles that from Latvia, Lithuania and Estonia.

Bronze continued to be imported and the same was true of iron, at least in these first centuries before the exploitation of native resources had been mastered. Most metal seems to have been imported as finished objects, and the evidence of native iron-working, slag in south-west Finnish graves, is all of the third century or later.

The grave finds represent the personal possessions of the dead; weapons, tools and ornaments which equipped the dead for a future life, whether in the grave or beyond it. The cremation burials do not preserve any organic matter, as grave goods were burnt along with the dead, and only metal objects and fragments of pottery survive, collected or scattered in the grave in such a way that one cannot tell what was the purpose of a brooch or pin. We know nothing of the clothing, and no cloth is preserved in the inhumation burials.

Fig. 25

The characteristic ornaments of the early Roman Iron Age are the eye brooch (so named because of the round holes in its upper part) neckrings with trumpet-shaped ends, and biconical spiral armrings; all are identical with other east Baltic and Esto-nian forms. Some jewellery of other provenance also occurs; heavily profiled brooches, S-shaped brooches, armrings and decorative pins, types found on the lower Vistula or further west, but not in Estonia. Only a very few ornaments come from Scandinavia, such as an electron finger-ring from Gotland and a brooch of insular type.

The weapons, single and double-edged swords, spearheads and shield-bosses, have their parallels in eastern central Europe, East Prussia, Bohemia and Silesia, and at least some of them were imported thence. How they came we do not know, as no graves with weapons are known from Estonia or the Vistula region at this period and our knowledge of weapon types in these regions is therefore scanty. But we note that the frequency of weapons varies in different Finnish cemeteries, the smallest quantities oc-curring in those whose other material is purely east Baltic. Twenty

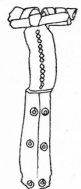

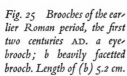

Fig. 25 Brooches of the earlier Roman period, the first two centuries AD. a eye-brooch; b heavily facetted brooch. Length of (b) 5.2 cm.

burials with weapons were excavated at Kärsämäki, usually containing only a spearhead and a shield-boss but sometimes a sword as well. From Koskenhaka come some excellent weapons, including a splendid shield boss and hand grip of bronze.

The most important tools are sickles and scythes, which show that the people were agriculturalists. Axes, knives, shears, awls, needles and an early strike-a-light (a natural stone with signs of use) are also found, and clay vessels naturally continued in use. Toilet articles are represented by one-piece bone combs and iron razors. Graves with weapons often include a rectangular belt buckle.

Plate 32

The Roman imports among the finds deserve particular attention and the most striking are two bronze wine ladles, one from Vähäkyrö in southern Ostrobothnia, the other from Laitila in Finland proper. The former bears on the handle the inscription 'L. Ansius Diodorus', which shows that it was made in Capua in southern Italy where a bronze craftsman of this name is known at the end of the first century AD. The other one may also be of Italian manufacture, or provincial Roman, which two bronze mounts for a drinking horn and the splendid shield boss already described certainly are. They probably came from the kingdom of the Marcomanni in Bohemia. Some Roman coins have also

Plate 34

73

been found, three silver *denarii* (now lost) and seven copper coins. The majority are stray finds and at least some of them are prob, ably secondary. Only two are from graves and therefore certain to have come to Finland during the Roman period. One is badly burnt, and the other, a coin of Hadrian (AD 117–138) also shows signs of burning. They were probably not buried before the third century.

As will be evident from the foregoing, our knowledge of the pre-Roman period is scanty and vague, although it is clear that the country was not uninhabited. So that when at the beginning of our era we find new, rich cemeteries and in them a new metal, iron, there can scarcely be any doubt that they are the relics of a new population who brought their own culture with them. Bur, ial custom and grave finds make it equally certain that they came from the area south of the Gulf of Finland, the greater part from north-east Estonia, the heart of the *tarand* grave area. Other re, gions also contributed, and the west coast of Estonia and Ösel have also been suggested. It is generally accepted that an immigration took place, and this is supported by the restricted area settled during the first two centuries, and by the gradual progressive colonization from west to east. Had it been a case of cultural influence alone, it seems likely that it would have affected a larger area simultaneously, and not proceeded one step at a time.

Some of the earliest cemeteries in western Finland continue in use up to the end of the heathen period, a time when we know from historical sources that the population was Finnish. It thus seems reasonable to regard those responsible for the first creation of these cemeteries as Finns, or at least their ancestors if we wish to restrict the term Finnish to the population that was formed in Finland itself. How important the previous population of the country was in this development can scarcely be concluded from the finds. They either blended with the new arrivals or (as Lapps) withdrew from them further and further north. It is clear that it was the culture of the newcomers which was decisive, but it may be necessary to emphasize that the immigrants arrived in small groups, with no suggestion of a 'conquest', and the process continued over many centuries.

It may seem strange that the cemeteries of the first two centuries are found on the coast of south-west Finland, and that there are none on the coast of Uusimaa opposite Estonia, except its extreme western corner. The eastern part seems to have been devoid of settled inhabitants during the Iron Age, and a possible explanation is that the people of the north coast of Estonia may have had traditional rights there so that colonists could not settle.

It is natural to seek economic reasons for the colonization, and the fur-bearing animals of the forests and the excellent fisheries of the south-west coast and islands unparalleled on the south side of the Gulf of Finland come to mind and provide another reason why it was the south-west coast which was colonized first. The first settlers were probably hunters and fishermen from the Estonian coast who, coming at first only seasonally, gradually stayed the year round and cleared fields, built houses and established a Finnish settlement. It would be a mistake however to assess the movement from a viewpoint exclusively concerned with the narrow perspectives of the Gulf of Finland.

The Roman Empire set its stamp on the centuries in which Finland was colonized, and in the last centuries BC had extended its authority across Celtic Gaul to England. At its greatest it included all southern and western Europe, its frontiers lying along the Rhine and Danube and sometimes further afield. The fortifications of the *limes* (the Roman imperial frontier) were no obstacle to trade; and for nearly two centuries (AD 30 to 192) Europe enjoyed the longest period of peace in its history.

New markets and communications brought a hitherto unknown increase in trade and wealth, with a corresponding prosperity to trading towns. Trade passed north and south across the frontier, to the north particularly along the river routes of the Vistula, Oder and Elbe. A particularly important intermediary between the Empire and northern Europe, including Finland, was the kingdom of the Marcomanni in Bohemia. Numerous Roman merchants and craftsmen established themselves there and the products of their industry flowed north along the convenient route offered by the Vistula. Within the Empire proper trade was encouraged by an excellent network of roads but outside it in the north men still had to rely on the natural waterways.

Statistics of finds from Scandinavia can give us some idea of the importance of Roman trade; about 500 bronze vessels and 280 glass ones of Roman manufacture, whether from Italy or the provinces, have been found in Scandinavia. They illustrate only one part of the Roman export trade, the lion's share of which was certainly consumer goods; wines, oils, spices, salt, cloth, etc., which have left no traces.

Finland was only indirectly affected by this trade which in the early Roman period followed the Vistula. In the first centuries of our era there thrived in the area round the Vistula a culture which has been called Gothic because Tacitus allots the area to the Germanic people of that name. From them cultural connections both direct and indirect crossed the Baltic to northern Estonia, south-west Finland and Scandinavia.

Pliny's account of a Roman knight's journey to the coast of Germania in the reign of the emperor Nero gives a historical account of Rome's connections with the Baltic. The purpose of the journey was to acquire amber to decorate the gladiatorial circus, and the route led from Aquileia at the head of the Adriatic to Carnuntum near Vienna, whence it was 600 Roman miles (900 kilometres) to the Baltic coast. This and other relevant features led most scholars to conclude that the 'coast of Germania' was East Prussia, Samland to be more precise, where amber has always been plentiful in the Kurisches Haff. Tacitus in his *Germania* mentions in connection with amber a tribe he calls the Aestii or Aesti whom he locates in this area. A large amount of amber was involved, as it sufficed to decorate the circus on a special amber day, and this suggests that amber was very important as an East Prussian export. It was obviously one of the cargoes which the merchants round the Vistula shipped south.

Another northern export was fur, some of which, according to Tacitus, was derived from animals of the outer ocean and the unknown sea (the Baltic?). The earliest historic account of fur trade in Rome is found in Jordanes in the sixth century, but there can be no doubt that it existed much earlier, at least as early as the period here mentioned, and it is by this trade that the colonization of Finland is linked with world history. Precious furs such as beaver, fox, marten and sable were used to buy objects of daily use from the south, and this explains the traces of the culture of the Vistula shown by the Finnish finds. Merchants from there travelled in Finland buying up furs, and some may have settled; and it was through them that influences from Rome, the Marcomanni and eastern Germania reached Finland. Wine ladles for instance are never found in the eastern Baltic and so certainly did not come from there; they must have come by a more westerly route which was most probably the Vistula.

The importance of hunting for the colonizers of Finland has been often stressed; one can say that in these first few centuries south-west Finland enjoyed its great hunting period, its *eräkausi,* just as the districts much later settled subsequently had theirs. The settlements were surrounded by large expanses rich in game, and finds show that hunting trips extended far into the wilderness. Oval strike-a-lights are frequent relics of these expeditions, and objects of this type appear to have been used over a period of many centuries, the earliest examples being crude natural pebbles from the very first centuries, and the latest beautifully finished rounded oval or rectangular objects made from quartz, quartzite, sandstone or slate, dated to the eighth century. Trials have shown that one can strike a spark to start a fire from one of these with a blow from an iron or steel edge. The stone was probably carried in the belt, as we know was the case in Norway. The number found in Finland exceeds 400, most as stray finds from inhabited regions, more rarely as grave goods. Stray finds are scattered over the whole country, including Karelia and Lapland, but these are not evidence of habitation but of hunting expeditions. Some may well have been lost, but the large number found in the wilderness has suggested that some may have been deliberately deposited as offerings to the gods by hunters seeking luck in the chase. Their wide distribution shows how important hunting was in the economy of the time. Fishing and seal-hunting served for subsistence as well as trade, though much of the colonists' food was derived from their own fields and flocks. Sites at river mouths and on river banks were probably favoured not only because of their better communications, but because it was easier to clear fields in such places. The nature of the agriculture is difficult to determine; the easiest way to clear woodland is by burning it, and the agriculture was probably not static, but a matter of clearing a patch by burning, cultivating it and then moving on and clearing another at the next stopping-place. This is perhaps the reason why so many of the cemeteries were used for such a brief period. It is possible that there was an area of more settled agriculture in south-west Finland, but even as late as the Middle Ages established fields are recorded only from Finland proper, Satakunta and southern Tavastia. The modern Finnish names of all the ordinary cereals appear on philological grounds to have been present already in proto-Finnic, and this suggests that the immigrants brought them with them to Finland, though archaeological evidence is lacking until the later Iron Age, when wheat, barley and peas are among the finds. Agriculture requires domesticated animals, and similar philological arguments suggest that the words for horse, cow, sheep, goat, pig and dog existed in proto-Finnic. Here again archaeological evidence is lacking even in the later period, but this is presumably because organic material has not been preserved in the soil of Finland, which is poor in calcium.

Whether or not the first immigrants made their own iron we cannot tell. All the iron objects are of types with parallels south of the Gulf of Finland or the Baltic, so that one cannot even tell whether the object was copied in Finland from a foreign model, much less whether its raw material was native. Later in the Roman period we find heavy iron slag, an indirect clue to iron-working and naturally enough that native raw material, 'marsh-iron', was being used.

The only historical source from the period which seems to relate to Finland is the description by Tacitus of the *Fenni*, a people he locates east of the Germani. This description of a primitive forest tribe does not accord very well with what we believe on archaeological and philological grounds to have been the culture of the Baltic Finns, nor with that just described, and it has often been held that Tacitus was describing the Lapps. It appears to fit the inhabitants of Finland before the arrival of the Finnish immigrants, whatever their race or speech may have been.

These first centuries are among the most important of Finland's history, for they saw the foundation of a nation that we can recognize as Finnish. Estonia has often, and with justification, been called the motherland of Finland, but even at this early date influences from further west played their part. The Gothic region mentioned above was one, and Sweden another, but it is difficult to know how much weight to attach to them. The single graves in Laitila on the other hand must be connected with Sweden, particularly Gotland, and both there and in Öland graves richly furnished with weapons also occur, like those of some Finnish cemeteries. There is nothing resembling them in Estonia or the Vistula region.

THE LATER ROMAN PERIOD (AD 200–400)

The settlement in south-west Finland continued during the whole of the Iron Age, and extended eastwards along the Koke-mäki river valley as far as the southern lake district of Tavastia, already within the Roman period. By AD 300 the settlement had reached Tampere and by 400, Hämeenlinna. By the end of the sixth century we find a cemetery in southernmost Tavastia and another on the eastern side of Lake Päijänne. The expansion was partly produced by people from the older coastal settlements, partly by newcomers from across the Gulf of Finland. Two rela/ tively short/lived cemeteries on the south coast of Uusimaa, at Siuntio and Porvoo may be attributable to these newcomers from the south.

Grave mounds from the period often show no recognizable structure, being made of stones and turf just thrown together, but some more regularly/built ones do occur. Square stone set/ tings have already been mentioned in connection with the *tarand* graves, and are reminiscent of a *tarand* cell. The latest of these extend into the fifth century. The grave mound from Siuntio mentioned above is round, with an outer edging of large stones, inner rings of stones, and a chamber/like arrangement in the middle. Both in situation and structure it is reminiscent of a Bronze Age cairn, but the finds which are scattered through/ out it are all from the third and fourth centuries. Burials of the same kind are found in Estonia at this period, particularly in Ösel, and the custom was probably introduced by immigrants from there. Another cairn of similar construction is found at Uskela, in southern Finland proper.

A round cairn at Soukainen in Laitila, made of large stones without earth filling, has an internal construction unusual at this period. Two separate stone cists orientated north/south were placed side by side on the original ground surface, each about 2 metres long. Their side walls were made from piled/up slabs of red sandstone, and each cist was roofed by a large flat slab. The mound, 10 metres in diameter, was then built round the cists which each contained a full set of weapons, and as no burnt bones were found, presumably originally an unburnt body. One of the graves was particularly richly furnished, for it

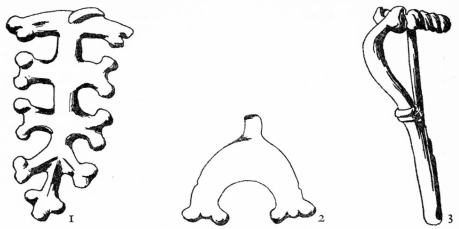

Fig. 26 Bronze ornaments of the later Roman period (AD 200–400). 1 Branched brooch; 2 crescent pendant; 3 fibula with returned foot. Length of (3) 8 cm.

contained as well as excellent weapons (a sword in a silver ornamented scabbard, a shield and two spearheads) a magnificent glass drinking horn and the remains of a provincial Roman bronze bucket of Hemmoor type. The two latter objects evidently came from the valley of the Rhine.

Plate 35

Contemporary parallels (the grave is of the fourth century) are found only in Gotland, and the cairn and its contents are clear evidence of close contact with Gotland. It seems most likely that the two men buried in the cairn were from Gotland, perhaps merchants, and the absence of women's graves may indirectly support this, as showing that the site was not a family grave.

The most important brooch-type from the third and fourth centuries is that with the foot turned upwards and backwards. It probably developed in the area north of the Black Sea and then spread in western, central and northern Europe, either through the agency of the Goths or through Roman trade; opinions about this differ. The type is represented in East Prussia, the

Fig. 26

81

eastern Baltic and in Scandinavia, and in the eastern Baltic region there are some local variants also found in Finland. Characteristically east Baltic are the so-called branched brooches, the large Estonian eye-brooches and brooches with enamelled ornament. The most striking form of the latter is the large horse-shoe brooch with enamelled roundels in the middle of the bow and at the ends. Hexagonal and octagonal armrings and crescent pendants are also found. It is no exaggeration to describe the ornaments of this period in Finland as eastern Baltic in character, but there are some pieces indicative of western influences, particularly gold neck- and finger-rings. The best example is the majestic neckring with animal-head ends from Nousiainen in Finland proper. Its closest parallels are in Scandinavia.

Plate 33

Other evidence for western connections is provided by the objects mentioned above from the grave at Soukainen in Laitila, the glass drinking horn, bronze bucket and weapons. The horn is comparatively large (12 cm. in diameter at the mouth) and is of colourless glass ornamented by blue and milk-white threads of glass melted onto it. The only directly corresponding one comes from Östergötland in Sweden, but this style of ornamental glass is represented by several cups elsewhere in Scandinavia. They are undoubtedly provincial Roman products, manufactured in the neighbourhood of Cologne, probably for Germanic customers; thence the imitation of a drinking horn in glass. The trade with Germania was an important one and it is interesting to see how far into northern Europe it extended by river and sea.

The Hemmoor-type bronze bucket is also provincial Roman, mass-produced in western Germany near Aachen. Many have been found in Scandinavia, though this particular one is unique in Finland. The weapons are also western and this is true not only of the Soukainen find but of weapons of the period elsewhere in Finland as well. Swords, spearheads and shield bosses show forms which occur frequently in the great Danish bog finds such as Vimose and Thorsbjerg, where the equipment of whole armies served as an offering to the gods. Where they were made cannot be determined. The richest graves of this period include a sword, two spearheads and a shield boss, but swords are rare, and only the richest and noblest individuals seem to have used one. The sword from Soukainen is distinguished from the others by having four grooves on the blade.

It is often difficult to decide how far the east Baltic objects are the consequence of trade and how far they are the personal pos- sessions of a newly-arrived immigrant, and this is particularly true of newly-established cemeteries. It is often uncertain whether they are to be attributed to the expansion of the earlier settlement or to quite new arrivals from overseas; this applies in particular to finds from the Kokemäki river valley and southern Tavastia.

During the later Roman period an enamel-working centre developed in north-eastern Estonia, of which the horseshoe brooches mentioned above are characteristic products. The art of enamelling came to Estonia from the Roman provinces, by way of either the lower Dnieper, or, as seems more likely, East Prussia. In Finland these enamelled horseshoe brooches are found mainly in the Kokemäki valley and the south-Tavastian lake district, with one additional example from Finland proper, and it has been held that they reveal an immigration from Estonia which brought both the brooch type and the art of enamel-working with it. At least one of the Finnish examples however seems to be of local workmanship, and so do one or two other enamels.

Plate 31

Enamel objects from the central area of settlement in south- west Finland are most easily explained as the result of trade, and the same applies to the east Baltic element in the area; it is a ques- tion of the import of actual metal. The Estonian trade visible here extends much further than southern Finland. We find traces of it in southern Ostrobothnia, and it is particularly marked in a north Swedish hoard from near Skellefteå in Norrland, which includes many east Baltic ornaments, some purely Estonian, and in particular two large enamelled horseshoe brooches. The find shows that traders (presumably fur-buyers) from the north coast of Estonia travelled far into the north over the Baltic and the Gulf of Bothnia. This was perhaps one of the foundations of the richness of the Estonian finds.

Western Finland had direct contacts not only with Estonia but with east Baltic regions further south, such as the flourishing region round Memel, but these were only occasional. The commercial importance of the Vistula region for Finland diminished considerably when at the end of the second century some of the Goths migrated to the area north of the Black Sea.

Objects from the western Roman provinces occur with increasing frequency in Scandinavian finds during the later Roman period, and the Rhine became progressively more important as a trade route to the North Sea. From its delta the route continued across the neck of Jutland to Själland and the Baltic, and places further east. Whether the trade was carried on in the Baltic by merchants from Själland or Gotland is unknown, though particularly in the northern regions it seems more likely to have been the latter. The grave from Soukainen mentioned above entitles us to give first place, at any rate as far as Finland is concerned, to trade from Gotland, and the trade in weapons shown by other graves seems also likely to have been negotiated through Gotland.

THE EARLIER MIGRATION PERIOD (AD 400–550)

At the end of the Roman Iron Age a new burial custom appears alongside the cairn, which continued to be the usual one. This was a cremation burial in a pit without any mound or marking on the surface above it. The richest of these is a grave at Hönsåkerskullen in Karjaa, western Uusimaa. The grave, dug near a large cairn, by a large stone, was only 50 cm. in diameter and 25 cm. deep, but contained no less than 6.5 kg. of burnt bones and a multitude of small finds (80 in all) including weapons and ornaments. Clearly two persons, a man and a woman were buried here: the ornaments were almost without exception east Baltic, the weapons show Germanic forms.

Similar cremation burials, individual graves with no surface mark of any sort, occur elsewhere in Finland during the early Migration period, and the type persists into the Viking period. The closest parallels to the Hönsåkerskullen grave, in richness of finds as well as in site, are to be found in western Estonia, where the well-known Kirimäe find included a cremation pit filled with burnt bones and over 150 objects. The grave is however the only one of its kind from this period in Estonia, and as few graves of the period have been identified nothing definite can be said about how far this type spread. In Finland cremation burials in pits have been considered to be borrowed from Scandinavia, particularly Gotland, and it has also been suggested that they are evidence of immigration from Scandinavia.

Grave mounds of this period are usually found either by themselves or in twos and threes. But both by the river Kokemäki and in southern Tavastia there are cemeteries comprising dozens of mounds, sometimes more than a hundred. Some are grass-covered mounds with a stone cairn inside, others simply piles of stones. It is certain that not all are graves, for burnt bones and grave goods are completely lacking in some, and the only finds are fragments of clay vessels, animal bones, iron slag and one or two metal objects. These mounds in fact seem to be rubbish-heaps, or other incidental traces of a settlement, but they are as yet insufficiently excavated for the situation to be clear.

Plate 39

The objects from the fifth and sixth centuries that have been found show that the basis of Finnish material culture continued to be east Baltic. Among ornaments of east Baltic character – and for the greater part of east Baltic manufacture – pride of place goes to the ring-decorated brooches, a late development of the brooch with returned foot. Also important are the brooches with spade foot, a type derived from the east Prussian star-footed

Plate 37

brooch. Some of the ring-decorated brooches are of silver, like those in Estonian hoard-finds of the period. Neckrings with thickened ends and armrings with segmental cross-sections are also common.

Alongside these east Baltic forms we find an increasing Scandinavian element. The most important western ornamental objects of the period are decorated with the so-called Germanic animal ornament, which is quite foreign to Finland. This, a characteristic sixth-century style known as Salin's style I, occurs most commonly in the North Sea region, in England and south Norway, but objects belonging to it have also been found in Sweden and Finland, particularly in south Ostrobothnia. Brooches, ornamental buttons, belt-buckles and mountings, and armrings decorated in this style are found in Finland. They were certainly imported.

Plate 38

It is during this period that the corpus of finds in Finland begins to show, at first to only a slight extent, an independent character of its own. There are some brooches of east Baltic type which show variations in detail, and a group of bird pins which can be regarded as particularly Finnish. They are the forerunners of the nature types which were soon to become dominant.

The importing of weapons from the west continued in the fifth and sixth centuries, and, as previously, the forms are all represented in the Germanic area, particularly in the Danish bog finds. We cannot point to definitely native forms, or even to evidence of native workmanship, though some forms from the end of the period may indicate that there were some native weapon-smiths. Shield bosses in Finland show an unbroken typological succession from the fourth to the sixth century, the earliest with a slightly rounded boss succeeded by ones with a pointed top, and these giving way to the spiked boss. It has sometimes been considered that they were made in Finland but no particularly Finnish type can be evidenced, and all the stages are paralleled in Scandinavia. At the end of the fifth century and in the sixth, graves with weapons often contain two spearheads which form a pair: they are both the same length with long sockets and short blades, one with an oval blade the other with barbs. The majority are found in coastal districts, which suggests that they are imported, but exact correspondences abroad are wanting, though similar examples are found. The possibility of native manufacture cannot therefore be excluded, though it must be remembered that the absence of corresponding forms elsewhere in Scandinavia may be more apparent than real: it may simply be because finds of any weapons of this period in Gotland are generally rare. It would seem likely that Gotland continued to play as decisive a part in the trade in weapons as it did in all other trades, partly because of the large number of *solidi* found in the island, and partly because of all the other evidence of its close contacts with Finland.

In Estonia (and sometimes in Finland as well) the period AD 400–800 is known as the middle Iron Age. The period, particularly AD 500 to 800 in Estonia, is much poorer in finds and much less completely known than either the preceding or the ensuing period. The large *tarand* grave fields with their extremely rich inventories go out of use at the beginning of the sixth century, and after this finds are few. It is obvious that there was a change of burial sites, but the graves which must have replaced the *tarand* graves have not yet been found, unless of course one supposes that the Kirimäe find described above represents the common practice, for which there is no evidence. It has been suggested that the reasons for the change were economic; as agriculture in established fields became the rule, replacing the earlier burning and clearing of patches in the forest, the earlier close unity of society was broken as collective effort was no longer so necessary and the individual could cultivate his own arable independently. The passing of land into private ownership also led to social differentiation within the community. This explanation is suggested by Estonian scholars. It might be argued on the other hand that the shortage of finds reflects a certain isolation of the eastern Baltic which set in at this time, perhaps caused by weakened or broken commercial connections with the south and west. The Germanic migrations led to the depopulation of vast areas, and the rapid advance of the Slavs in the middle of the millennium also must have interrupted earlier communications. During the fifth and sixth centuries the elongated grave mounds attributed to the Kriviches appear on the south-east shore of Lake Peipus, and only a little later the cone-shaped mounds of the Slovenes appear round Lake Ilmen and Volchov.

This inevitably affected the situation in Finland, and indirectly lent increased importance to connections westwards. This must be borne in mind in considering the emergence of Finland from the previous phase of material culture dominated by east Baltic influences, into one of independence.

Though Scandinavian objects are numerous in the finds from the fifth and sixth centuries, they are scattered through the cemeteries. They occur together with east Baltic forms, and not a single grave with purely Scandinavian material is known; not even the cremation pit burials have a wholly Scandinavian inventory. There can be no question of any Swedish colonization; at most there may have been a quite insignificant trickle of immigrants. The Scandinavian objects extend over the whole inhabited area to the eastern outskirts of the settlement of Tavastia. That shows that they are the result of trade.

The fifth century and some decades before and after it are characterized in Sweden and Denmark by large amounts of gold found in hoards of varying composition – coins, rings, and ornaments. The large islands in the Baltic, Gotland, Öland, and Bornholm, are especially rich in Roman gold coins, *solidi;* the finds from the Swedish mainland are mainly in the form of rings and ornaments. The largest of these finds, from Södermanland, weighed almost 13 kg., so it will be seen that very considerable amounts of gold were involved.

The multitude of coins from the islands, 250 *solidi* from Gotland, and 200 from Öland, suggests that they were at least partially accumulated through trade and that Gotland continued to
play an important part in trade. Some of the gold in Scandinavia
came with returning participants in the wars of the migration
age, and derived ultimately from the imperial treasuries of Rome
or Byzantium, whether it came into Germanic hands as dane-
geld or plunder. The half-century 476–526, the time of Odoacer
and Theodoric, seems to have marked the peak of this activity.

The flood of gold of this period did not reach Finland, with
the exception of south Ostrobothnia and Åland, where a sword
pommel of gold filigree is a slight token of it. Precious metals in
general were rare in Finland in the early Iron Age. The east
Baltic ring-decorated silver brooches, one or two Scandinavian
silver brooches, and the rim of a sheath make up all the silver
known from Finland.

To conclude this chapter on western Finland two finds which
show Scandinavian activity in an eastward direction may be
mentioned, one from the island of Tytärsaari in the Gulf of Finland and one from the island of Riekkala off Sortavala in Lake
Ladoga. The first includes a magnificent equal-armed brooch
with Germanic animal ornaments, buckles and belt mounts
with animal-head and human-head motifs, burnt bones and
sherds of pottery. It was found in the island's sand dunes. The
other comes from a modest cremation burial, and contained
two open armrings with thickened ends, two ornamental buttons with animal ornament and a spiral finger-ring.

The forms of the objects from Tytärsaari point to Sweden, as
there are no corresponding pieces from western Finland, so that
they cannot be derived from there or from the south coast of the
Gulf of Finland. The belt fittings suggest Gotland, where the
closest parallels are to be found, and the burial evidently reflects
the presence of Swedish seafarers, who may have been merchants
or pirates. Tytärsaari lies about halfway between the south coast

of Finland and the mouth of the Narva, providing an ideal base for piratical descents on the eastern Baltic. Scandinavian sagas tell of such enterprises at a somewhat later date; King Yngvar of Sweden was killed in Estonia, and his son subsequently led another expedition to avenge him there. The Tytärsaari find cannot of course be connected with any particular historic event, but an explanation along similar lines seems likely.

It is also probable that the find from Ladoga can be attributed to Swedish ventures to the east. No traces of any population on the north coast of Ladoga, or indeed from Karelia as a whole, are known at this time, and whilst the presence of some inhabitants archaeologically undetectable and not metal-using is feasible, it seems much more probable that the man buried in Riekkala arrived by ship. The types in it are rare in western Finland, and foreign to the eastern Baltic and north Russia, and can only have reached Karelia by sea.

THE LATER MIGRATION PERIOD (AD 550–800)

The justification for drawing the line between earlier and later Iron Age in Finland at *c.* AD 550–600 is that an independent Finnish culture begins to emerge at about this time, and is clearly reflected in the finds. Types unknown outside Finland now become dominant and the genuine Finnish cremation burial without mound dominates other burial customs. This development of national forms did not involve any isolation, and cultural and commercial contacts were never richer in the Iron Age than in the seventh and eighth centuries.

The inhabited region in western Finland continued to expand. Many new cremation cemeteries developed during the seventh and eighth centuries and continued in use throughout the rest of the Iron Age, succeeded after AD 1000 by simple burial of the dead. These large grave fields represent a more fixed and intensive settlement than the earlier cairns, probably a society with permanent fields and estates. At this period some separate settlements developed further east and a cemetery of west Finnish character of the end of the eighth century has been found on the western shore of Lake Ladoga in Karelia. The first Iron Age cemeteries in Åland are from the sixth century.

The new Finnish type of grave, cremation burial under level ground, is without any mark on the surface save a few stones sticking up amongst the grass. The cemeteries are large, running into tens and hundreds of square metres with from one to four layers of stones. Below, between, and sometimes above the stones the remains of funeral pyres were scattered over centuries, and burnt bones, ashes, grave goods, and fragments of the same object may be scattered many metres from one another. The stone patterns clearly developed gradually as the remains of each new cremation were scantily covered with new stones.

Plate 40

The photograph we reproduce shows what these stone-settings looked like. The distinction between this and a cairn is really that the cairn rises distinctly above the level of the surrounding ground, and covers a more restricted area. The borderline between the two types can be rather vague, and sometimes a setting of this kind might equally well be described as a low cairn. The true cairn continued in use as the second most frequent burial form in south-west Finland right up to the beginning of the Viking period, and in the lake district of Tavastia right up to historic times. It is natural that the central regions should be most advanced along the line development was to follow, and their denser settlement would produce a different type of burial from that appropriate to an isolated pioneer settler. On the other hand each individual farm does seem to have had its own cemetery even in areas of densest population, and some of the modern villages in Finland proper have several grave fields on their land.

Plate 37

Sometimes a closed find, all the objects in which were deposited at one time, can be found in these cremation cemeteries.

Plate 41

The way in which the ashes and objects are kept together varies; they may be in a boat, a cauldron, or simply a hole in the ground; occasionally isolated inhumation burials are found inside the area of a cremation cemetery.

When the small churchyard belonging to a hamlet in southern Finland proper, Yliskylä in Perniö parish, was extended in the 1890s an inhumation cemetery from the end of the heathen period came to light. In addition a low grave mound of stone and earth was discovered, covering a very rich boat grave (a cremation burial) on the original ground level.

Apart from burnt bones, the find included six shield bosses, fragments of several shield handles, four swords (all bent), five spearheads, four knives, metal parts of a belt and about nine hundred rivets. The objects were mixed in charcoal and ashes over an area about 80 cm. across. Some of the rivets were packed in shield bosses, and the weapons had been broken to take up less room. The objects date the grave to about AD 600.

The large number of rivets shows that it was a boat burial, and from them it has been calculated that the boat must have been about 15 metres long. Whether the dead man was burnt in the boat, or whether the boat was simply one part of the grave goods provided for him cannot now be determined, but Finnish folk poetry contains many descriptions of a dead chieftain being burnt in a boat, and the remains of boat and pyre then being buried in the earth. This would support the first alternative, and so would the contemporary boat burials in Sweden whence the custom spread to Finland. In Finland the form was adapted to fit the traditional cremation, as indeed had often happened in Sweden and almost without exception was the case in Norway.

In Sweden boat burials in the strictest sense, where the dead were buried unburnt in a boat, are known only from Uppland and in one instance from Blekinge. The Uppland burials are of men, and evidently it was the head of the clan who, generation after generation, was buried with this rite. The wealth of the clan

is reflected in the rich grave goods, for the dead man is accompanied by his splendid weapons, his horse, dogs and a good
store of food, household goods, drinking vessels and quite
often a sort of draughts board. The objects show connections,
direct and indirect, with central as well as western Europe. How
far the burial custom itself is derived from the older Uppland
chamber tombs, how far an introduction influenced by the *Rei-*
hengräber, the Germanic graveyards of central Europe, is difficult
to say. The traditional interpretation of the boat as intended for
crossing the river of death has been recently rejected in favour of
the more mundane view that it was simply one of the everyday
requirements with which the dead man was furnished for his
new life.

The most famous group of boat burials, at Vendel in Uppland, has given its name to the whole period (AD 600–800) in
Sweden. But boat burial continued in Uppland through the
Viking period and up to the eleventh century, and the same is
true of Finland. The number of boat burials in Finland is difficult to establish, as they cannot always be identified with certainty; rivets may indicate only coffins or other wooden objects.
Only a very large number of rivets of varying sizes is sure evidence of the remains of a boat, particularly in the graveyards containing unmarked burials under the level surface in which most
of the boat graves are situated, and the clench-nails and grave
goods are often widely scattered, so that one must wonder whether
old boats may not have been used as fuel for the pyres. There
are however at least twelve certain boat graves from the Finnish
mainland, and at least another thirty from Åland. Those on the
mainland are mainly on the coast, two in south Ostrobothnia.

Two cremation pit burials are worthy of special mention.
They are at Käräjämäki in Eura, Satakunta. The name means   Plate 46
'Thing mound' and the graves are actually within the so-called
'Judge's ring' of the old assembly-place. Käräjämäki is one of
the richest inhumation cemeteries in Finland, with a large num-

93

ber of graves, the oldest from the sixth century, the most recent from the end of the heathen period. Apart from these graves, visible on the surface as shallow oval depressions, two grave mounds are situated on the ridge on top of which lies the judge-ment-ring. It consists of twelve large stones in a ring. According to received tradition a thirteenth stone called the 'Chief's stone' used to stand in the middle of the ring. The ring is 8 metres in diameter, and the two cremation pits, both of them shallow burials of the seventh century, were inside it.

Tradition tells us that this 'Judge's ring' was the site of a local assembly, and appears to be supported by the name Käräjämä-ki. The sources tell of open-air court places even in historic times, and Olaus Magnus depicts the 'Judge's ring' in ques-tion on his *Charta Marina* of 1539. He describes such meeting-places in his *Historia de gentibus septentrionalibus* (1555) and says that open and lofty sites in the forest were used for purposes of justice, administration and counsel. Verdicts were given by the king's reeve and appointed magistrates. Nevertheless the circle of stones seems in the first place to have been a grave, as many similar 'Judge's rings' in Sweden have shown themselves to be. They are rare in Finland and only one survives apart from that at Eura. When the grave ring was first used as an assembly place one cannot say; but it was probably back in the heathen period, as some of the references in Finnish folk poetry to assem-blies in circles evidently refer to this kind of ring.

At the end of the sixth century a radical change in burial rite took place in a small area in Satakunta (in Eura, Köyliö and Yläne parishes) where the dead were buried unburnt. Several cemeteries have been found in which the unburnt bodies are buried in graves in more or less regular rows. The graves are shallow, only 20 to 60 cm. below the top soil, and about 1 metre apart. The orientation varies, being at first usually north/south or north-west/south-west, but later becoming east/west. The graves often include remains of a wooden coffin or at any rate some sort of wooden covering for the dead. The dead were buried fully clothed and equipped with all their weapons, tools and ornaments. Sometimes there is an arrangement of stones in the soil filling the grave or above it, with soot and charcoal among the stones; at other times the grave includes potsherds, slag, and clay discs which evidently belong either to some magic rite or the funeral feast.

This new type of grave cannot be derived from the occasional burials of unburnt bodies known from earlier phases of the Iron Age. It must have been produced by influences from abroad, but as yet no one has been able to demonstrate clearly whence they came, and why they are confined to such a restricted area. There are inhumation burials without mounds on Gotland at this date, but they are characterized by limestone grave chambers; the Upp-land boat graves are also inhumation burials, but there the boat is the important feature. There are also inhumation burials round Memel, in the south of the eastern Baltic region, but none are known from areas between there and Finland.

The central European Germanic cemeteries arranged in rows come into the picture again at this point. The dead were buried unburnt, well-equipped with grave goods and often in wooden coffins, all features which recur in the Finnish graves. Some have wished to explain the Finnish graves as due to their influence, imagining that some newly-arrived group, perhaps a warrior band, introduced the custom. On the other hand the objects from these graves are not very readily distinguishable from those of the rest of south-west Finland, and they cannot really be said to form a separate cultural region. The question of the origin of these graves must therefore remain open.

Inhumation burial spread to the rest of south-west Finland only in the eleventh century under Christian influence. Graves of this period are dealt with in the later section on the transition from heathenism to Christianity, the time known in Finland as the crusading period.

Finds of dwelling houses from the period are still lacking, but alongside the grave material we have certain finds from the old forts which complete our picture of the later Iron Age. These forts are found in all the inhabited parts of Finland apart from southern Ostrobothnia, but are as yet almost uninvestigated, so that we cannot say when the earliest was built. It is, however, certain that they existed in the Viking and crusading periods, and some may have been fortified before this. A gilt brooch of the sixth century with Germanic animal ornament was found on the fortified hillock of Vanhalinna (the name means 'the old fort') near Turku, which has been regarded as the predecessor of the historical Turku castle. The brooch shows that the place was being visited in the middle of the millennium, and the steep hill may have been a place of refuge even before it was fortified.

Plate 65

The old fortified places of Finland are usually steep and inaccessible hills or mounds, sometimes islands, which offered good natural defences. The gentlest slopes and most easily accessible places were furnished with stone ramparts which have survived at least in part to our own day, though often levelled. Sometimes the top of the hillock was artificially steepened. It seems likely that the rampart was surmounted by a timber wall, but these have long disappeared and one can only guess at their height. The stone ramparts are often many metres across, with a height of one or one and a half metres. They are built of unfinished stone, with no bricks or mortar, which in Finland always indicate a structure of the historic period. Excavation of the rampart of Rapola in Tavastia revealed holes and transverse channels which evidently marked the original position of the lowest cross-beams in low timbered chambers which were filled with gravel and broken stone to make a foundation for the timber wall proper, and provided a walk round the inside of it. Many of the forts have elaborately protected entrances, often so arranged that anyone entering must do so diagonally, presenting his right hand side (unprotected by his shield) to defenders on the ramparts. The actual entrance was narrow, and could be closed by a gate of planks.

Similar ancient forts are found in the east Baltic region, Russia and Scandinavia. They differ in detail and also in use. In general one can regard them as places of refuge for the populace, particularly when they are located in inaccessible regions. In Finland they do not seem to have been continuously inhabited, and certainly cannot be regarded as fortified towns. Sometimes nevertheless remains of buildings have been found in them, and these were perhaps the dwellings of the watchmen. If one supposes that the forts formed part of a continuous chain and the occupants signalled from one to the other in case of hostile threat – a theory for which there is some evidence, – then they must have had permanent watchmen if not garrisons.

To some extent at least the forts seem to have been built against invasion from abroad. In Finland proper a chain of them runs along the coast as if protecting the inhabited area against attack from the sea. In the Kokemäki river two fortified islets controlled river traffic and could prevent an enemy penetrating inland. The forts in the lake district of southern Tavastia appear to form a defence line along the watercourse, and in Karelia there are many ancient forts on the north shore of Lake Ladoga. In all these areas there are in addition many forts belonging to isolated communities.

Once the practice began of burying the dead unburnt, we can form a much better idea of how ornaments and metal details of the dress were worn. Even the garments themselves may be partially preserved by the oxidized metal, and we can distinguish which objects indicate men's and which women's graves. The graves show that from the later Iron Age onwards women's dress consisted of a long loose gown, fastened at the shoulders with a pair of brooches joined by a chain across the breast. These shoulder brooches are important for dating, as they regularly changed in appearance. The introduction of brooches of these kind must

Fig. 27   Ornaments of woman's dress, Finland (AD 600-800). Length of equal-armed
shoulder brooches 4.5 cm.

Fig. 27

have given a Scandinavian look to Finnish fashion which it had
not had previously. In the eastern Baltic region the breast chain
was still worn between two ornamental pins. The characteristic
women's ornaments from the period AD 550–800 are small equal-
armed shoulder brooches, one so-called crayfish brooch worn in
the middle of the breast, a short chain, and armrings with broad-
ened ends made of thin bronze foil, concave-convex in shape.
This combination is constantly repeated in the grave finds. The
brooches are derived from Swedish examples, but have been
modified in Finland, and are easily distinguishable from the
Swedish form.

    The frequent use of different kinds of rings as ornaments is an
east Baltic feature. Neck-, arm- and finger-rings all occur frequently, and some of the pins and brooches are also east Baltic
in form. How far these were made in Finland and how far imported is difficult to tell. Some are so common that they must
have been made locally. The particularly Finnish forms with no
foreign parallels show that the manufacture of these ornaments
was carried on in Finland, and it is natural enough that both
Swedish and east Baltic types were imitated. Fashion preserved
to a large extent its east Baltic character.

The genuinely Scandinavian brooches are surprisingly few when one considers how important Swedish originals seem to have been in the development of native types. Some oval tortoise brooches, one or two round brooches with animal ornament and belt buckles of good quality should be mentioned. Closely linked with Finland is the serpentine-looped brooch. Its distribution includes Gotland, central Sweden and Finland, but it is more frequent in Finland than in the other two areas combined. Its origin is to be sought on the continent though the execution is north European. The garnet-ornamented ones at least must be imports, though the others may be of local manufacture.

Germanic animal ornament of the seventh and eighth centuries is in Finland best represented on weapons. It was particularly the age of the parade sword with bronze hilt often gilt or silvered and decorated with animal or plaited band ornament. The ring-swords are particularly splendid. The type takes its name from the typologically earliest example, from Kent in England, where a loose ring hangs from the pommel. Ring-swords were widely distributed over the whole Germanic area. Eventually the ring was cast in one piece with the pommel, and in the end it became no more than a swelling on one side of the knob. This final stage is represented by two Finnish examples, and as it is unknown outside Finland it has been concluded that they were made in Finland. If that were so, one would have to assume either that foreign craftsmen had settled in Finland or that Finnish craftsmen had been trained abroad in some Germanic region. When one compares the ring-swords with other bronzework from Finland it does not seem very likely that they are native work; if they are, it is odd that no equal skill is found in the bronze ornaments. There are also three sword hilts in the form of squatting beasts which have no direct parallel outside Finland; the same considerations apply to them as to the ring-swords. Other sword-types cannot be mentioned in detail save for one from

Plate 44

Plate 42

about AD 800 in which the whole handle, the grip as well, is entirely of bronze. The most beautiful example of the type has the whole grip ornamented with figures of birds and animals in slightly sunken oval fields, and is clearly Gotland work.

Investigation of the origins of these swords is made more difficult by the possibility that blade and hilt were made in two different places. The damascened blades, made of steel and softer pure iron, which gave them an elegant rippled finish as well as added elasticity, are certainly from western Europe. The large number of swords with animal ornament in Sweden, particularly at Vendel and Valsgärde, has led to the hypothesis that they were made there, and animal-ornamented swords in Finland have often been said to be of Swedish origin. In fact one can scarcely use animal ornament as evidence of the place where a sword was made any more than of the nationality of the man who made it. Many of the blades were made on the continent and the men who ornamented them were probably a cosmopolitan band who had served an international apprenticeship. The craftsmen nevertheless seem to have worked from some sort of drawings, and at least in the seventh-century style, Salin's style II, which is disseminated over the whole Germanic area.

The greater part of the weapons, swords, spearheads and shield bosses of the period AD 550–800 are types found all over Scandinavia, and evidently of central European origin. Alongside them however we find some types unknown elsewhere but very frequent in Finland and these may properly be regarded as specifically Finnish. The most important are the so-called 'angos', barbed spearheads with a long neck, others are dagger-like spearheads, funnel-shaped shield bosses, straight-backed heavy knives (saxes) with bronze grips. They show a high standard of skilled working, and this suggests that some of the weapons in the commoner international styles might also be Finnish copies.

Plate 43

The inventory of the seventh- and eighth-century weapon graves often includes a large iron pin shaped like a shepherd's crook, intended as a cloak fastening, and also various metal belt mounts. The heavy iron belt buckle with round mounts and escutcheons which has been found in a few graves is west European. The small bronze belt mounts on the other hand are from eastern Europe, from the Kama area; they include cross-shaped, elongated, three-armed and shield-shaped forms. The graves often contain bridles and bits and occasionally a whip handle or rattle; this latter consists of a socketed or tanged iron rod with a hole or eyelet for a leather thong. There is often a metal ring running through the hole, with strips of metal on it which rattle when the staff is shaken. Many scholars have attributed magic significance to it, and compared it to the ring-staff which has an almost world-wide distribution. These objects are common in Scandinavia, particularly in Norway where there are hundreds of them. They are also associated with the Viking-period in Finland.

In general one can say that as far as weapon-types are concerned Finland belongs to the Germanic world. At the beginning of the period fairly heavy equipment (a sword, a saxe, two spears, a shield with funnel-shaped boss) was usual. Later the shield bosses became lighter and at the end of the eighth century they disappeared altogether from the finds; at the same time we find only one spear instead of two.

At the beginning of the seventh century a group of Germanic kingdoms had established themselves in western and central Europe, forming a continuous zone from the Lombards in Italy to the North Sea and the British Isles. At the same time pressure from Slavonic peoples was moving the eastern frontier of the Germanic peoples to the north and west, and this was very important as far as conditions in the Baltic area were concerned. It was suggested above that this probably explains the scarcity of finds from AD 500–700 in Estonia, and it seems also to have interfered with the southern trade connections of Denmark. Trade with the west was not affected, and the Limfjord was an important trade route from Baltic to North Sea, with Born-holm once again an important rendezvous.

Uppland and Gotland stand out as the richest areas of Sweden and it has been assumed that Gotland at this period or somewhat earlier became politically connected with the Svea Kingdom. One sign of this is the Scandinavian activity in the eastern Baltic shown by the Grobin cemeteries on the west coast of Latvia. One is a large cremation cemetery of perhaps a thousand graves unmarked on the surface and certainly of Gotlandic origin. The others are two grave fields with mounds of central Swedish type. The whole complex covers the period from about AD 650 to 850 and thus reflects a long-lasting Scandinavian colonization east of the Baltic; scholars have seen in it a Gotlandic trading colo-ny and a Svea garrison. These colonies – whether trading or political conquest is involved – show the increasing power of Gotland and Uppland on the Baltic, and are an overture to the Viking period's expeditions eastwards. It is natural to enquire how far similar activity was directed against Finland. No sign of any similar Swedish settlement has been found in Finland, and nothing indicates Swedish political domination either. As long as people regarded weapons of the Vendel culture, partic-ularly those of Salin's style II, as specifically central Swedish or Uppland, there was a natural tendency to assume that Swedish influence or perhaps occasional settlement was shown by such types in Finland. Some even used to talk of Swedish suzerainty. But if the weapons of the Vendel culture are international trade goods, and Germanic animal ornament is not restricted to Upp-land, Sweden's role becomes much less than was assumed, and is best discussed in terms of trade relations and cultural influence.

The resemblance of Finnish arms of this period to the com-mon Germanic ones, and the new burial custom of inhumation without cremation found in a small area of Satakunta, have been variously explained. The phenomenon may be seen as the in-troduction of the Vendel culture into Finland, or as direct evidence of immigration, or as the return home of warriors who had taken part in campaigns on the continent. It has been suggested that among these immigrants were the master craftsmen who formed the Finnish weapons and gave them their general air of continental common style. And finally, some have been ready to see a *herrenklasse* of natural rulers coming from the continent. The grave goods, however, in these new Satakunta inhumation burials resemble so closely those of other contemporary cemeteries in western Finland that they do not even suggest any great social difference, let alone a distinctive ruling class. Nor does it seem very plausible that master craftsmen should be confined to one very restricted region, as immigrants may have settled anywhere. The reason for the assumption that some smiths must have arrived from abroad is to be found in the high quality of craftsmanship found in the native weapons. These cannot be international trade goods as are the common Germanic types, but must have been made locally, and they are of such high quality that it seems difficult to explain them as produced by purely local workmen. The skill they show involves at least training by foreign example.

The greater part of the weapons found are not of this kind, but were certainly imported, and the question arises whether the importation was direct, by continental merchants journeying to Finland, or whether it was carried out through some local entrepot, perhaps Gotland. The finds are indecisive and views differ. But the finds from Grobin show a Gotland activity in the eastern Baltic that can scarcely have tolerated competitors, and the Vendel culture seems to have been firmly established in Gotland before it was in Uppland; as the Swedish scholar Nils Åberg has put it, 'There is nothing to show that the Svear in Uppland partook in this development from the beginning, but the finds make all the clearer the extent to which they harvested the eventual crop. The first initiative seems to have been in Gotland and Öland, perhaps in Bornholm and Skåne as well.'

Alongside the increasing western trade, Finland's connections with the east, with central and eastern Russia, also increased. Other objects from the Kama region, as well as the 'Permian' belts and mounts, have been found, in the shape of silver neck-rings and pendants. The main import from central Russia was certain axes.

During this period, from AD 500–700, a flourishing culture existed around Perm and Vyatka in the Kama region, which possessed luxuries such as Persian silver bowls and some Byzantine ones as well. This silver was clearly got by fur-trading. Finds in northern Russia show that fur buyers and merchants from Kama journeyed far to the north, at least as far as the banks of the Pechora, to buy up furs. When one sees the evidence of their intensive activity in the north, it seems natural to assume that it was they who brought the 'Permian' belts to Finland. Corresponding pieces are not known from the east Baltic regions, with only one unimportant exception, and it seems that the trade route passed to the east of these lands. The trade seems to have been at its most active in and after the second half of the seventh century and it continued during the Viking period. That it was an initiative from the east is suggested by the fact that though we find the 'Permian' material in Finland, no corresponding Finnish material is found at Kama.

The sixth-century *solidi* of the eastern Roman Empire found in Gotland are assumed to have reached there through the kingdom of the Gepidae in Hungary, and there is other archaeological evidence for contact between Hungary and Scandinavia. This contact was weakened but not destroyed by the invasion of Hungary by the Avars at the end of the sixth century, and seventh-century material from Finland suggests contact whether direct or indirect. The line of the Dnieper-Dvina across Latvia and Estonia has been suggested as the most likely route, but it is quite possible, of course, that Gotland served as an intermediary.

The east Baltic forms show continual contact with Estonia, and for the first time some of the material found in Estonia is of Finnish origin and shows Finland as the donor and Estonia as the recipient. From the end of the period, about AD 800, we find signs of direct contact between Finland and the Memel area.

The most eastern imported object of the period is a mount showing a crouching Bactrian camel, probably derived from the trade with Kama. The most western is an Irish cross-shaped mount, gilded and decorated with spiral ornament. It presumably came through Sweden where imports from the British Isles can be clearly demonstrated.

A Finnish folk-poetry description of the cremation in a boat whose remains were subsequently buried was quoted above in discussing boat-burial (p. 92). There are some other descriptions which can be combined with archaeological detail, and there is thus reason to attribute some of the folk poems later included in the Kalevala to this period. Some of the common themes of the poetry were already known, as a mount from Sweden proves by its depiction of Väinämöinen fishing for the sea-queen Vellamo's maiden. This gives us a concrete example of the way a story-theme can wander. It can spread out over a wide area, just like Germanic animal ornament. Finland at this time provided a field of activity for itinerant ornamental metalworkers, skilled weaponsmiths, and poets, and the many-facetted culture of the period was shaped by all three.

CHAPTER VI

The Iron Age in South-West Finland after AD 800

THE VIKING PERIOD (AD 800–1050)

Fig. 28

THE VIKING AGE brought a great change to the Baltic, and the new economic situation naturally affected Finland; but this did not involve any break or sharp alteration in culture as reflected in material objects, and development proceeded smoothly. National ornamental forms predominate and some ornaments whose originals were Swedish are modified and developed in a way which clearly distinguishes the Finnish ones from their models. The small equal-armed shoulder brooches are now replaced by round brooches with a central cross, decorated with serpentine animal figures which twine themselves over and under the arms of the cross. The animal is derived from Germanic animal style but in Finland this motif develops in the direction of geometrical stylization and becomes at last a starkly formalized linear ornament. At the same time the brooches are decorated with projecting knobs, as many as twelve on later examples. The type developed in western Finland and survived throughout the whole Viking period, with such clearly marked development that no less than six stages can be distinguished. About twenty examples have been found in Sweden (though the earliest stages are not represented there) and some are found south of the Gulf of Finland.

The round brooch with pierced ornament in the shape of Carolingian lions is one of the typical forms of the ninth century in western Finland. Horseshoe brooches are very common, as they are all over the Baltic area during the Viking period, and are found in many different forms, including one with facetted and knobbed terminals which may be regarded as particularly Finnish. It is found outside Finland, but not very frequently,

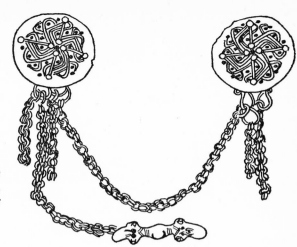

Fig. 28 Ornaments of woman's dress, Finland (AD 800–1050). Diameter of round shoulder brooches about 6.5 cm.

and the knob design is so usual and characteristic in other Finnish ornaments from this period, that it can be taken as a sure guide to Finnish provenance. It occurs also on the equal-armed brooches often worn on the breast in the Viking period.

The multitude of ring ornaments is an inheritance from the east Baltic culture, but the forms are now overwhelmingly the specifically Finnish ones. Ornamental chains are frequent, and there are numerous pendants, of which only the so-called bear's-tooth amulets can be mentioned. They are made of bronze, but are imitations of real animals' teeth and are frequent in south-west Finland.

Plate 45

Only a fraction of the large variety of ornaments has been mentioned. It forms the basic theme which is enlivened by less common variations and by imported objects. The common characteristic of the native ornaments of the ninth and tenth centuries is that they are heavy and solid bronze castings. Most were clearly made by village craftsmen, and the execution is mediocre. A complete set of ornaments must have been a fair weight to wear. The complete inventory of a woman's grave included plaited neckrings, pearls, solid armrings, brooches and decorative chains; and some items of clothing, the cloak, apron and head-

Plate 47

dress, were usually ornamented with bronze spirals often in complicated patterns. The decoration of clothes with metal is found
in the eastern Baltic as well, particularly in Latvia, but in a different technique, and the custom is unknown in Scandinavia.

This wealth of bronze is naturally a sign of prosperity, for it
had to be imported and paid for. Precious metals are either rare
or entirely absent, and it is only in eleventh-century graves that
silver becomes commoner. The only noteworthy silver object
from the ninth–tenth century is a thistle brooch of the type
traditionally called Norse-English, and that was an isolated find,
not from a grave.

At the beginning of the Viking period the native manufacture
of weapons seems to have been in decline; only one solitary type
of spearhead can be regarded as specifically Finnish. The stan-
dardization of weapons in the north, caused by the dominance
of the rapidly expanding arms manufacture of the Rhineland
and south Germany, had its effect in Finland as much as elsewhere. Most of the swords of the Viking period were certainly
imported; this is true of the damascened blades, often bearing a
Christian inscription or cross, and signed by the maker's name
Ulfberht or Ingelried. Ulfberht swords are very common, and
as much as one third of the Viking swords of Finland would
appear to have come from this factory which must have been
active over many generations.

It is of course quite possible that the damascening technique
was known in Scandinavia as well, where so many finds of pig-
iron and smith's tools show an active iron manufacture, and
there are signs that it was known at least on Gotland. The
sword blades were also often fitted with handles locally, thus
Plate 53   acquiring a regional character. A good example of this is the
group of swords whose hilts are silvered and ornamented with
animals in the rune-stone style. The ornamentation on these has
been said to be characteristic of Gotland; from there they were
brought to Finland.

Sword and spear remained the most common armament. Shield bosses on the other hand became scarcer. This need not necessarily mean that shields were no longer used, but perhaps only that they were made entirely of wood, as we know from Latvian finds was the case in the eastern Baltic. This is a difference from the state of affairs in Sweden, where iron shield bosses remained usual. From the tenth century onwards the broad-bladed Viking axe often occurs in graves and it continues into historic times, at least to the beginning of the twelfth century.

A general description of the culture of western Finland in the Viking period might be that it was a prosperous and stable peasant culture. Pure luxuries are lacking, precious metals scarcely found, but the heavy solidity of the bronze ornaments reflects farmers who were comfortably-off, as do the imported weapons. People were well able to afford expensive things if they were wanted, and everything points to a flourishing trade.

The Viking expeditions eastward, and the routes which they opened across Russia to the Arab world and Byzantium, expanded European trade. The Baltic was no longer a cul-de-sac but opened onto far-reaching and very profitable trading opportunities. Trade centres developed in the Baltic region to which streams of riches and imported goods flowed from east and west; some of them, such as Birka and Hedeby became famous, and distributed goods far and wide. Birka in particular was of great importance for Finland. It is Sweden's oldest town, first mentioned in 876 in Rimbert's biography of St Ansgar, the Apostle of the north, who preached there in the middle of the ninth century. It lay on the island of Björkö in Lake Mälaren 30 kilometres west of Stockholm. The remains, with a surrounding city wall, a cemetery of over 2500 mounds, and a citadel, show that a most impressive and flourishing town existed here, from about AD 800 to 975. The rich and diverse finds throw much light not only on the prosperity of the inhabitants but also on their far-reaching commercial contacts in east and west.

The Viking ventures eastward probably followed the same route as trading vessels did some centuries later according to a Danish itinerary of the thirteenth century. The journey started from central Sweden (Birka), heading eastwards past the Åland islands and passing south of them, thence past the Kökar and Jurmo islands to Hitis, and then on past the southernmost tip of Finland, Hankoniemi, to Porkkala west of Helsinki. From there ships either followed the south coast to the head of the Gulf of Finland, or turned south to Tallinn and continued along the Estonian coast to the mouth of the Neva. It was possible to navigate a river-route from Viipuri, at the north-east corner of the Gulf, to Lake Ladoga, but anywhere further, such as Volchov in the south or Onega along the Svir, was better reached by the Neva route.

Finland's geographical position on this great route to the east was of great importance, and obviously stimulated Finnish trade in the Gulf of Finland. New trade and trading places no doubt developed on the south coast. Inhabitants of Tavastia had very good communications with the coast along the rivers and one can assume that at least the people of the south journeyed down to buy and sell, perhaps on particular market days when foreign merchants came. Archaeological finds from the south coast are certainly few but they do not come from any settled habitation; people only went there to fish or trade. Some graves near the frontier may be connected with this activity, and some small coin finds in western Uusimaa also reflect it. Coin finds are much more common on the south coast of the Gulf of Finland, which suggests that this side was more used than the north as a route.

Trade routes from east and west joined in Birka, and alongside them lay Gotland where about 690 silver hoards show how close its connections with the Arab world were. When Birka was deserted, in the eleventh century, Gotland became the leading commercial centre of the Baltic, as Birka's successor Sigtuna was unable to preserve its dominance.

This Swedish activity is reflected in the so-called Viking colonies of the eastern Baltic and the great Russian rivers. Some of
the former are both named in historical sources and archaeologically located. Grobin on the west coast of Latvia has already
been mentioned, and others are Truso near present-day Elbing
and Wiskiauten on the Kurisches Haff. In Russia the nearest to
Finland was Staraja Ladoga (Old Ladoga) the Aldeigjuborg
of the sagas, about 12 kilometres south of Ladoga on the Volchov. The earliest settlement there seems to date from the seventh
century and to have been Finno-Ugrian; by AD 1000 the
inhabitants were clearly Slavonic. Many Swedish objects are
included in the finds from the ninth and particularly the tenth
century, the most notable a wooden stave with a runic inscription, and it is certain that Swedes lived there or at least visited
the place, though whether they were a real colony, or a garrison,
or some chance sojourners we cannot be sure. The real importance of the site was that it controlled one of the Vikings' main
routes to the south, as it was possible to get far enough down the
river system for boats to be pulled a short distance overland to
the Dnieper. Staraja Ladoga must have been very important to
Karelia, and so was the culture which developed on the south-
east shore of Lake Ladoga. There are many cemeteries with rich
grave goods, largely Scandinavian, and many scholars have concluded that there must have been some Swedish colonization of
the area. The mounds that have been investigated, however, have
also produced objects which must be classified as Finno-Ugric,
and the graves themselves have features not typical of Sweden.
The usual view now is that they show a local population of
Finnish origin whose wealth of Swedish material was the result
of trade and the introduction of metal-working techniques to the
region. Much the same may also be true of the regions west and
north of Lake Ladoga (p. 136).

There is ample evidence in the finds of the large part played
in western Finland's trade during the Viking period by Birka

and central Sweden. There are twenty equal-armed brooches, oval brooches, and armrings decorated with wavy lines or plait- ed, all of which are Scandinavian, and valuable clues to the size and direction of the traffic, even if they are not to be regarded as imported trade goods in the same sense as salt, spices and other consumable goods which have left no trace in the finds.

In the light of all this it seems natural to assume that the trade in weapons was also conducted through Birka. The animal- ornamented scabbards came from Sweden; so may the swords they contained, which had central European blades, have done. In the eleventh century Gotland probably served as the inter- mediary, but in the Viking period Gotland material is absent from Finland, and the distribution of some sword types points to Birka. Swedish objects occur in most of the large cemeteries of western Finland, but during the Birka period they seem to be concentrated in the north of Finland proper, the present parishes of Laitila and Kalanti. This region clearly had particularly close contacts with Birka and central Sweden, and local peasants sailed their own boats to Stockholm well into historic times. The route from this region to the valley of the Kokemäki river with its dense settlement went to the great bend in the river, as the river's lower course seems to have been uninhabited, perhaps because the lower reaches are fast-flowing and navigable only with difficulty. The route continued from the Kokemäki river valley to Tavastia.

Objects showing contact with Finland proper have also been found in Birka. West Finnish pottery indicates that Finns lived in the town and made pots there, and some Finnish bronze ob- jects have been found in graves. It is natural enough that a town of Birka's size should draw material from a large hinterland, and also that it should attract craftsmen from abroad. Opinions about the origin of Birka vary, some attributing it to Swedish kings, others to Frisian merchants. Frisians, the famous merchants from the mouth of the Rhine, indisputably journeyed to Birka as the life of St Ansgar tells us, confirmed by the large number of imports from western Europe. Whether the Frisians got any further, to Finland, is much less certain.

Some place-names have been put forward as evidence that they did; for example, those including '*pirkka*' (birk) or '*kugg*'. The value of the first depends on the assumption that 'birk' is originally a Frisian legal term, the origin of the town-name Birka, and not simply the Swedish natural description 'birch island'; there is no unanimity on this. Place-names involving 'kugg' occur along the south coast of Finland, and have been derived from the name of a type of Frisian trading ship, the cog. The Kugghamn at Birka probably was so called already during the Viking period, and has been cited as evidence that the 'kugg' names in the Gulf of Finland may be as old, and similarly con-nected with Frisian trade. But it has been maintained that these names can scarcely be older than the historical period and thus cannot tell us anything of pre-medieval trade. On the other hand Gotland picture-stones show the ship type in question, a round single-masted ship of high freeboard, evidently already familiar in the Baltic before the Viking period, and thus not necessarily Frisian. Archaeological material gives no conclusive answer to this debatable question of Frisian trade in Finland. The difference which emerges from a comparison of the material from Birka with that from Finland may help to throw some light on the question. If central European merchants had the same direct contact with Finland that they had with Birka, one would expect the same sort of western European imports in both. We find such agreement in weapons, but western European glass, gold and silver, Rhineland pottery, Frisian cloth whose presence in Birka is so significant, are all absent from Finland, and this evidence, though negative, makes it seem unlikely that Frisians reached Finland. There are no Frisian coin-finds from the Viking period either, the earliest being one of the end of the eleventh century from Karelia.

Nor does the archaeological material suggest that Finns (except for those in Åland) took any part in Viking expeditions, even those to Russia. The rare coin finds from the north coast of the Gulf of Finland are no more than fleeting traces of Vikings passing by. The Arabic coins found in west Finnish graves and hoards obviously arrived in the north as a result of Viking activity but it is not necessarily to be taken for granted that they were brought back from raids by Finnish participants returning home. With the exception of a small hoard from Perniö in south-western Finland proper we know of no hoards on the mainland consisting exclusively of Arabic coins as do those of Åland (p. 133). Another point is that there are no finds of Finnish character along the Russian river routes; the so-called Varangian colonies there produce material typical of mainland Sweden, and the picture is not significantly altered by the isolated Finnish round-brooches from north Russia.

Contacts with Estonia seem to have been weaker at the end of the ninth and beginning of the tenth century than they had been earlier. A certain community of taste survives, but direct imports from Estonia are difficult to demonstrate, and characteristic west Finnish objects are completely lacking in Estonia. It is difficult to say whether this is because Finland was now turning more to the west, or because communications across the Gulf of Finland were interfered with by the Viking traffic along it. Contact evidently became closer again about AD 1000.

The Viking period was one of expanding settlement in Tavastia. The newly settled areas lie east of the mother region, round Päijänne and even further away. Cemeteries of west Finnish character are found near Mikkeli in Savo dating from about AD 900, and isolated finds, as well as one or two graves, are known from many parishes in this province and in easternmost Tavastia. They mark one stage in the settlement, and the same phase of expansion is reflected by the Viking age cemeteries of Karelia the oldest of which may be as early as AD 800 (p. 134).

With the depopulation of the districts of southern Ostrobothnia inhabited in the Iron Age, the whole region became dependent on the Kokemäki valley. No new settlement took place in
it until historic times and only stray finds left by travellers are
known. Some graves have however been found in between the
old inhabited district and the Kokemäki valley, and they may
represent an attempt at colonization. Most seem to have come
from Satakunta, but a few may have come north from Tavastia.

THE CRUSADE PERIOD (AD 1050-1150)

The description of the Iron Age in west Finland brought us up
to the end of the Viking period, and to the last century for which
archaeological sources alone are available. This last period is
known in Finland as that of the crusades, and ends in Finland
about 1150 though in Karelia not until the end of the thirteenth
century.

It is characteristic of the period that inhumation now completely ousted cremation everywhere in western Finland, though
isolated cremations are still found on the frontiers. The first inhumations took place in the old cremation cemeteries, but new
inhumation cemeteries were soon started on sandy hills or slopes,
sometimes alongside the old cremation cemetery, sometimes in a
new spot.

The dead were usually buried in wooden coffins in graves 60
cm. deep. The older orientation was north/south, but west/east
or south-west/north-east soon became the ruling one; the head
was at the west or south-west end so that the face was towards
the rising sun, which agrees with Christian usage. The graves
are clearly distinguished from Christian burials however by their
very copious grave goods, not only clothes and ornaments but
weapons, tools and domestic implements. It is not until the middle of the twelfth century that grave goods disappear.

The earliest inhumation burials often include a layer of stones

Plate 54

over the coffin, a memory of the stone cairn of an earlier period, but perhaps also intended to prevent the spirit of the dead from rising again. In some cases one can point to other features which certainly go back to heathen burial customs. In a cemetery at Nousiainen near Turku, cremations with heathen grave goods lie on top of inhumation burials and must be later than these. The grave goods included bracteates from as late as the twelfth century. It is only natural that burial customs should have been rather unstable in a transitional period between heathenism and Christianity.

The most important finds from this period are the textiles. One characteristic feature of Finnish fashion in the later Iron Age has already been mentioned, the use as ornament of various Plate 57 bronze spirals either sewn onto the cloth or woven into it. The oxidization of the bronze has preserved so much of the cloth that reconstruction of the womens' clothing of both west Finland and Karelia in the crusading period is quite possible. Her attire consisted of a woollen shirt, skirt, apron and cloak. The shirt had long sleeves and was fastened in front with a brooch, and was usually of simple stuff with single warp and weft; the skirt, fastened on the shoulders, was usually of quadruple twill, and had a decorated border. The apron was rectangular, and like the cloak and headdress decorated with bronze spirals; but it was the decoration of the cloak that received most attention, beginning in the actual process of weaving, as bronze spirals were interwoven with the plaited warp threads. An appliqué band on either side then left the ends of the warp as a fringe. Other shapes, stars and crosses were applied in bronze. The married woman's headdress was a hood with a border of bronze rings, whilst the unmarried girl had a simple head band.

Men's graves have produced shirt, smock and belt, but as male clothing was not decorated with bronze it has not been so well preserved. It is certain that cloaks were used and presumably some sort of long stocking or tight trouser can also be assumed.

The belt was usually of leather, fitted with bronze buckle, strip mounts and end tags. Though most of the surviving cloth is wool, it is probable that linen was more usual than would appear – it rots very quickly. Garments were dyed with native herbs, and whilst one cannot exclude the possibility of foreign imports such as Frisian cloth, self-sufficiency in clothing does seem to have been complete. The only surviving foreign fragments are of brocade, and were found in Karelia.

Small horseshoe-shaped brooches of bronze or silver were used, almost without exception, as shoulder or breast brooches. One common characteristic distinguishing the grave goods of this time from those of the Viking period is that the decorations are now smaller and lighter, and silver occurs more commonly. This wealth of silver is also reflected in a group of hoards of the period.

These hoards, about thirty from west Finland, belong to the period between 1020 and 1100. They consist mainly of western European silver coins, though Byzantine and Arab occur as well; most are German or Anglo-Saxon. Broken silver and silver ornaments are included as well as coins. The largest find, from Nousiainen near Turku, includes 1476 whole and 221 fragmentary coins as well as a large number of silver ornaments. The composition of the hoards has been interpreted as showing that the silver came from Gotland. Western coins flowed into Gotland by many routes, and this provided the background for the combination of coins we find in Finnish and Swedish hoards at this date. The proportion of German, Anglo-Saxon and other coins is the same in finds in both Sweden and Finland, so that the Finnish hoards are yet another testimony to the dominance of Gotland trade in the Baltic.

It is perhaps desirable to point out that no real use of coins is known in Finland in prehistoric times. It was the weight of metal that was decisive, and in graves from the end of the Viking period and the eleventh century we find small balances and

Plate 56

weights, like those of a modern apothecary, for weighing precious metal. One such has been found in Lapland (p. 147). The
broken coins of both graves and hoards also show how even
minted silver was weighed to get a given sum.

Hoards of this kind are not necessarily signs of prosperity.
They are usually regarded also as signs of war and disturbance,
particularly when a large number occurs in the same district at
the same time. If we take this view of these finds, then the eleventh
century in western Finland must have been full of troubled times,
and one might also cite a rune-stone from Gävle (Sweden) as
evidence. It says that Brusi carved the stone in memory of his
brother Egil (Ihil), who fell in a raid on Tavastia. This was a
raid under a certain Freygeir, and Egil probably led the con-
tingent from Gästrikland. The stone has been dated to 1030–
1050, early in the period of the hoards.

Apart from the hoards the numerous imported weapons, particularly the splendid swords which must have cost a very considerable sum, suggest real wealth. The commonest sword is a
general European type with a flat round pommel. A special
variant of it is represented by a magnificent sword from Eura
with a guard which is broader towards the ends and decorated
with three roundels. Both pommel and guard are adorned with
inlaid silver wire in palmetto, spiral and leaf patterns. The same
type of ornament is found on some spearheads and axes, but a
more usual type is represented by a group of swords in which
pommel and guard are silvered and then decorated with incised
serpentine animal figures in rune-stone style as well as palmettos.
The decoration is worked in niello, and is also found on the
sockets of some spearheads. The sword blades are of continental
workmanship damascened or decorated with inscriptions and
symbolic figures. The most famous has on one side the inscription DEUS MEUS and on the other a row of symbols, a falcon,
a bishop's crozier, and a glove. The sword blades were probably
provided with their handles in Gotland, where the spearhead

Plate 55

Plate 52

sockets were ornamented, and these too show how, after the decline of Birka, Gotland dominated the Baltic. Its trade-goods also included belt-buckles and mounts, and ornaments.

In some graves in west Finland, and also in Karelia (p. 142) we find a cross or crucifix worn on a neck chain, and the deceased had presumably been baptized even though they are buried in a lavishly heathen fashion. Most of these eleventh-century crosses are forms widely distributed in the north of Europe, and many of them are evidently of Scandinavian workmanship. They have been found only in men's graves, and it may be that it was only widely travelled men who came into contact with the new faith and were baptized. It is possible however that Christianity was preached in west Finland at this period. The burial-rite of inhumation is a result of Christian influence, and these inhumation burials with lavish grave goods have sometimes been called 'barbaric Christian', sometimes simply 'Christian'. If by Christian burial we mean burial in accordance with Church ritual and without grave goods, then it obviously is inapplicable here. On the other hand a transition to purely Christian graves is perceptible in some of these cemeteries, and occasionally they lie so near medieval churches as to make it seem that the Christians built their church and churchyard on an earlier cult site of which they had been able to get possession. A papal bull of 1229 shows this when it confirms the Church in Finland as owner of those pagan sacred groves and cult places which were presented to it by newly-converted heathens. The so-called 'offering-stones' (p. 120) show that cult site and burial ground often went together.

Plate 62

The inhumation burials with grave goods include no other unmistakably Christian objects apart from the pendant crosses, and they may contain a heathen miniature axe, symbol of the thunder god, as well; clearly, other beliefs can alone account for the bear's-tooth amulets, either genuine or metal imitations, which also occur. All this is natural enough in a period of transition, and it must also be remembered that a grave does not necessarily reflect a dead man's beliefs, but rather those of his surviving relatives, so that a dead Christian might well receive a heathen burial from his relatives, or *vice versa*. The occurrence of some burials without grave goods does not mean that the whole population of a district had become Christian; that can be concluded only when burials are confined to consecrated ground.

In this connection the well-known silver hoard from Halikko in southern Finland proper deserves mention. It consisted of a crucifix and two simple crosses on splendid chains, all of silver, a round pendant ornament and 36 large filigree-decorated beads also of silver. They were found in a plain clay pot, probably concealed during some disturbance. It has been suggested that the silver was part of a bishop's treasury, whether deposited here in the course of early missionary activity or as booty gained by the plunderer of a church.

Memories of heathen cults survived long after the so-called first crusade (about 1155), which united the country to Sweden and brought about the establishment of a firm ecclesiastical organization in Finland. Stone axes and chisels from the Stone Age have been found in some Iron Age graves, and were evidently believed to have magic powers. Similar 'thunder hammers' are still used by the superstitious in our own century to cure disease or avert fire, and other similar superstitions have survived in Finland.

Plate 66

In many Iron Age cemeteries in Finland proper, Satakunta and Tavastia, so-called 'offering stones' have been found. These are rocks or stones fast in the earth with round depressions hollowed out in their top. These cup-marks are 4–10 cm. in diameter and 1–4 cm. deep, and the number occurring together varies from ten to sixty. The earliest are in cemeteries from the beginning of our era, the latest date from well into the historic period. Their position in the cemetery connects them with the cult of the dead and this is confirmed by tradition. Cult-place and grave field went together. Tradition has also preserved (even up to our own day) memories of their connection with a fertility cult and in the nineteenth century offerings for good crops were still placed in them. Placing offerings in them to guard against sickness is probably a secondary development, but it too is mentioned in documents from the eighteenth century, though sacred springs were more often connected with health. It took a long time for the Church to eradicate these superstitions, and many traces of them are found in tradition and folklore.

CHAPTER VII

The Iron Age in the rest of Finland

SOUTH OSTROBOTHNIA

THE PART OF south Ostrobothnia inhabited in the Iron Age is very strictly limited to the region east of the town of Vaasa, and amounts to only five present-day parishes. The neighbouring coastal parishes lack all signs of settled population during the Iron Age for the very natural reason that the present coast was then not yet above water. The rapid rise of the land-level has affected the landscape much more in this region than in southern Finland, and it is therefore particularly necessary to stress that, appearances notwithstanding, its Iron Age population was a coastal one, whose cultural connections were mainly across the sea.

The earliest Iron Age finds here as in southern Finland date from the first centuries of our era. The typical grave of the early Iron Age is a regular round cairn of stones with no earth filling, about 10 metres in diameter and 2 metres high. It is elegantly dome-shaped, often with a central stone and an edging of large stones. Cremation is the dominant rite, and the primary burial is usually on the south side of the central stone. Secondary burials, which are quite usual, are as a rule out towards the edges. The resemblance to the Bronze Age mounds is obvious.

The circular and rectangular arrangements of stones at Latjineliden in Vöyri form a group on their own. They have an edging of large stones with a filling of earth and small stones inside it. The structure is reminiscent of a cell of a *tarand* grave, and is indirect evidence of east Baltic influence. The cemetery started about AD 200 and continued in use for several centuries.

The resemblance between Bronze Age and Iron Age mounds in south Ostrobothnia has led some to put great stress on the continuity of the population between these two periods. This is certainly possible, but should not be taken for granted. In south Ostrobothnia as in southern Finland, there is no continuity of finds to bridge over the blank centuries before the beginning of our era. Finds from the first two centuries AD are very rare; they include an east Baltic neckring with trumpet-shaped ends, the Capuan wine ladle mentioned above (p. 73), an S-shaped brooch, and an armring and branched brooch from the Vistula. It is hopeless to attempt to deduce from these whether we are dealing with an immigration or with cultural borrowings of new shapes and a new metal. The distinctive form of grave found at Latjineliden might show the arrival of a small number of new immigrants, and points, directly or indirectly, to the eastern Baltic as their place of origin. It may be significant that the oldest Iron Age object from Ostrobothnia, the neckring with trumpet-shaped ends, would be at home in that region, but it does not of course rule out the possibility of a continuity between Bronze and Iron Ages. There is a striking difference between the Iron Ages of south Ostrobothnia and southern Finland. The former does not show signs of any progressive expansion, whereas the latter shows a continuing colonization through the centuries.

Whatever attitude we take to this material, whether we see it as evidence of immigration or cultural borrowing, we must consider whether the influence from the eastern Baltic is likely to have been exercised directly, or mediated through southern Finland. Both are possible; the find at Storkåge shows that in the later Roman period the Ests had journeyed much further up the Gulf of Bothnia than in south Ostrobothnia, and they may well have done so earlier. Neither the wine ladle nor a somewhat later provincial Roman bronze bowl can have come from the eastern Baltic, where Roman bronzes are quite unknown. Wine ladles are found both in southern Finland and in Norrland, the Swedish province west of the Gulf of Bothnia, and the one in question may have arrived via these regions. But it seems more likely to have come from the Vistula, and there is nothing against direct contact between that area and south Ostrobothnia; indeed the branched brooch mentioned above would support such a theory.

During the third and fourth centuries the material from south Ostrobothnia is mainly east Baltic in character, and in part resembles that from southern Finland, though there are differ-ences as well. There are no brooches with returned foot or enam-elled brooches, whilst the branched brooch of east Baltic form is almost a national type. The few objects certainly Scandinavian include a silvered swastika-shaped brooch, and a bronze sword grip, perhaps from the Trondheim area of Norway whose con-nections with south Ostrobothnia are further illuminated by fifth- and sixth-century material. The only imported object from western Europe is a provincial Roman bronze bowl, evidently made in the Rhine valley in the fourth century. It must have come to Finland by a more westerly route than the wine ladle, probably by way of Zealand and Gotland. This was probably also the route taken by some Germanic forms of weapons.

Outside the inhabited area proper are many coastal mounds whose dating is uncertain. A few contain eastern objects alien to the south Ostrobothnian culture, and they may belong to an aboriginal population scarcely represented in the archaeological evidence. A cairn in the interior is probably the grave of a new colonist from the central area of settlement, as its grave goods resemble those current there. It is of a type found on the islands and lake shores of the interior, called *lapinraunio*, 'Lapp cairns'. They do not usually contain grave goods and cannot be dated; the one mentioned above, at Viitasaari is exceptional.

The fifth and sixth centuries saw a growth of prosperity in south Ostrobothnia. The material shows an unbroken develop-ment; there is a large eastern Baltic element resembling that in south Finland, brooches with ring ornament, brooches with spade-shaped foot, etc., but some local types develop which give the culture a character of its own; equal-armed brooches whose middle has longitudinal facets and flared sides, brooches with

convex relief lines and facetted knobs, brooches with a trian-
gular foot and attached pin, and other types. They are found only
rarely outside south Ostrobothnia and give its culture a more
individual air than south Finland can claim at this date.

Comparison of Ostrobothnia with southern Finland at this
time also shows that Scandinavian forms are more frequent in
former region, particularly objects with Germanic animal ornament, but others as well, including some of silver. There are
even about twenty-five of gold, quite unknown at this period in
southern Finland. They are mainly finger-rings or currency
rings, but at least seven gold coins have been found, of which
four are preserved. They date to AD 408–491, one from the western Empire (Valentinian III) the others Byzantine (Theodosius
II, Leo I and Zeno). The total weight of all the gold finds is
scarcely 100 grammes; compared to the wealth of gold in Sweden
they are insignificant, but it must be remembered that these south
Ostrobothnian finds are from graves, whereas the Swedish ones
are mainly hoards, so that comparison with Sweden is scarcely
legitimate. A truer comparison is with the culture flourishing
west of the Gulf of Bothnia, with its centre in Medelpad and
Hälsingland. It is very relevant to south Ostrobothnia and therefore deserves some description.

This culture appears already in the fourth century, from which
we have one or two graves and isolated finds, but like south Ostrobothnia it reaches the height of its development in the fifth and
sixth centuries. This 'Norrland kingdom', as one scholar has
called it, developed under very strong influence from Norway,
and its connections in the fifth century with south Norway and
in the sixth century with the Trondheim region were quite decisive for it. Economic factors seem to have played a large part
in this, as south Norwegian mercantile activity was involved in
North Sea trade.

During the sixth century this Norrland culture expanded
both north and south, and its contacts with south Ostrobothnia

were naturally close. Importation from Norrland is therefore the most likely explanation of the presence of most of the Scandinavian material in south Ostrobothnia.

So much weight has been given to this by some scholars that they have interpreted it as evidence of colonization, and seen south Ostrobothnia as entirely passive in this transfer. But there is an evident continuity in culture, and as there is no expansion of the inhabited area there is no evidence of any new immigration. Obviously some individuals such as merchants, fur-buyers, and craftsmen may have arrived, and certain Finnish archaeologists have considered that the evidence is consistent with the existence of Swedish colonies or chieftains in south Ostrobothnia. The Scandinavian appearance of some of the material by no means proves this: it might equally well be explained by the arrival of a few skilled craftsmen.

The Scandinavian element in south Ostrobothnia comes not only from Norrland; some of the objects are of southern type, reminiscent of Gotland and unknown in Norrland. The rarity of gold is typical of Norrland as well as of south Ostrobothnia, and what gold they have could be a trace of Gotland trading activity, though in both the main trade route probably went west to Norway rather than south to Gotland.

The prosperity of Norrland was short-lived, lasting not more than two centuries before vanishing. That of south Ostrobothnia survived a couple of centuries longer, but then ceased in the same mysterious way. One can scarcely be wrong in attributing both their prosperity and their subsequent apparent depopulation to the economic circumstances relating to a trade of some sort, and this trade must obviously have been in furs.

The occurrence of objects of specifically Ostrobothnian type in the Kokemäki river region and even in south-west Finland shows that communications between south Ostrobothnia and southern Finland improved during this period. The improvement continued during the seventh and eighth centuries and

there seems to have been a real levelling-out of cultural differences. The most striking evidence of this is the occurrence of
cremation burials under level ground in Ostrobothnia, but there
is a growing similarity in objects as well, and most of the Finnish
brooch-types appear there. Two boat burials, both cremations,
are the richest finds of the period in south Ostrobothnia. A warrior's grave at Pukkila in Isokyro parish is distinguished by its
splendid grave goods which closely resemble those from Vendel
in Uppland. It is clearly a chieftain's grave.

Another important discovery is the marsh find from Levän-
luhta in the same parish. Human bones and some seventh-century material were found while draining and later excavating
the sump of a waterlogged pasture. Remains of fifty-two individuals were found as well as animal bones (horse, cow, various
birds) and some metal objects, among them a bronze cauldron,
fragments of a silver ring, seven armrings, a serpentine-looped
brooch, and a garnet-decorated bronze button. The ages of the
deceased varied widely, from children to fifty-year-olds, of both
sexes. The average male height was 158 cm., the female 147 cm.
– much shorter than later Iron Age skeletons in south Finland.

The find is probably a sacrificial site. Various interpretations
have been suggested, notably that it was a burial place probably
reserved for lower-class people or slaves, but nothing comparable exists.

The relatively precious goods would seem to tell against
the theory that the dead were slaves, but these objects might well
be sacrificial offerings, as were the animals whose bones are
found. The people were also sacrifices. Human sacrifice in Finland is mentioned only once, much later, in a papal bull about
the inhabitants of Tavastia in 1237, but Germanic sources of
various dates mention human sacrifice, and there is archaeological evidence that it took place in Scandinavia.

To the west of Gulldynt in Vöyri, one of the richest cemeteries
in south Ostrobothnia, remains or at least traces of a settlement

have been excavated. They are so scanty that they give no clear idea of the buildings, though these were certainly made of wood. But traces of any kind of building on the mainland of Finland from this period are so scarce that their very rarity entitles them to mention.

Only one or two grave finds from south Ostrobothnia belong to the end of the eighth century, and after AD 800 they cease altogether. Indeed a progressive decrease in finds is noticeable from about AD 600 onwards, and only one or two significant finds are known from the Viking period, during which the old settled area seems to have been abandoned. A very recent hoard find from Vähäkyro includes Arabic silver coins, the latest of AD 842; this suggests we must qualify our assumption, as it can scarcely be other than the hoard of a local inhabitant of the mid ninth century. The Arabic coins are obviously connected with Viking ventures in the east, just beginning at this period, but that does not explain their presence in the hoard or how they got to south Ostrobothnia. When the Viking age decisively opened the new routes to the east, the Gulf of Bothnia and its narrows lost their economic importance, and this presumably explains their depopulation, as people moved to more advantageous areas. The first traces of west Finnish settlement in Karelia came from this period, and the two movements may be connected. It has also been suggested that the depopulation might have been caused by the attacks of outside enemies; the folk-tale battle between Kalevala and Pohjola, ending in the latter's defeat, might preserve a memory of this with Kalevala representing the people of Satakunta. It must be stressed however that the depopulation was the result of a long-drawn-out process lasting a century, not of any sudden blow. It cannot be proved from the archaeological evidence that there never was a battle, but it should be pointed out that the evidence does suggest close and friendly contact between south Finland and south Ostrobothnia during the seventh and eighth centuries.

The Bronze Age was succeeded in Åland as it was on the main-land by a long period in which finds are very rare, and this period lasted into the sixth century in Åland, longer than it did else-where. Few objects are known from there and they cannot be exactly dated. On the south of the main island of the Åland group is a small cemetery with chamber-like arrangements of stones, whence come pin fragments which might be pre-Ro-man, and some apparently Bronze Age graves on the open coast lie so low down that the places cannot have been dry land before our era, though no datable objects have been obtained from them.

In any event these finds show that Åland was not completely depopulated after the Bronze Age. Some survivors hung on, fishing and seal hunting, until they blended with the newly arrived Iron Age settlers in the sixth century. The remains of these immigrants, their graves and house sites lie near the present settlements, and almost every old Åland village has some such remains within its boundaries. The graves are mounds of sand piled over a central cairn of stones, and vary greatly in size, from a diameter of 2 metres to 20. The mounds are often surrounded by an edging of stones and sometimes topped by a memorial stone or a round 'sun' stone. The burials in these mounds are always cremations; the dead were burnt on a pyre and the remains of the pyre were then spread on the original ground surface and covered by stone and sand. The burnt bones, or a part of them, are gathered into a clay vessel. The large number of boat rivets in the graves shows that boats were burnt on the pyre, and prob-ably many of the graves are true boat burials in which the dead man was burnt in his boat.

In the groups of grave mounds are also found the so-called 'triangles' or arrangements of stones in the form of elongated triangles with straight or concave sides, and also some of the ship-settings of stones. These do not usually contain graves and are either cenotaphs or cult sites. The rectangular mounds edged

Plate 48

with stones, and filled with earth and small stones up to the level of the edging, are very distinctive. Their contents have largely disappeared, but traces of inhumation were occasionally found in them. Some of these graves date from the end of the heathen period, when cremation had been abandoned, and inhumation adopted under Christian influence, though the dead were still buried in the old family cemetery.

About 380 Iron Age cemeteries are known from the main island of Åland – the smaller islets are devoid of them. The ten thousand separate grave mounds are found in ones and twos as well as in groups of over a hundred. They cover a period of five centuries from AD 500 to 1000 and many of the larger cemeteries were in continuous use over the whole period. They were the cemeteries of one family or one farm, as appears from the fact that a present-day hamlet may have many such on its land. Parallels to these burial customs are to be found in Sweden, particularly central Sweden, where similar round mounds, triangles, ship-settings and rectangular mounds with stone edgings are all to be found. There are no corresponding forms in mainland Finland, and the grave forms are certainly Swedish.

Plates 49, 50

House sites on Åland are rectangular stone enclosures of raised ground, often grouped together. The walls were made of vertical poles between which twigs and brushwood were interwoven and caulked with clay. Post-holes in pairs inside the building show where the roof pillars stood. Some of the houses were divided into two rooms by a partition wall, and one of them may have been a cattle byre though it is more likely a separate kitchen, as the farms consisted of several buildings and surely had the cow-house separate from the living quarters.

The door is usually in one of the long sides. Sometimes the long walls are convex, and the plan is almost like an oval with cut-off ends. Nothing definite is known about the construction of the roof, apart from the post-holes of the roof pillars which suggest a longitudinal roof beam, and the roofs may have been thatched with straw or turf. The typical sites are quite large, often more than 20 metres long and 7 or 8 wide, but in groups of this type traces of smaller cottages were sometimes found which may have been small timbered huts. The oldest datable site is from the seventh century, the latest from the historic medieval period; that is to say they appear together with the grave mounds and, like them, have no precedent on the island; they can be taken as typical of new immigrants. Parallels to the house sites are difficult to adduce, for though many of their features are found in Scandinavia, so few sites in central Sweden, where one would expect the closest resemblances, have been excavated, that it is impossible to make detailed comparisons. The 'warrior graves' (in reality early Iron Age house ruins) in Gotland and Öland have the outer walls marked by a solid stone foundation, but were lean-to structures, not wattle-and-daub framed buildings. The few remaining sites from the Finnish mainland are very ill-defined and difficult to interpret but seem most likely to have been timbered cabins.

Among Åland's other antiquities of the Iron Age are to be noted six forts of the same kind as other prehistoric northern forts; steep rocky crests whose most accessible sides have been fortified with stone ramparts, lying apart from the habitation sites and evidently intended as refuges. Some have a kind of forecourt, others only a plain rampart, and the outwork is a feature pointing west to Sweden as it is unknown in mainland Finland, where the plain type is found as in Åland.

The oldest Iron Age burials are from the sixth century, and among the objects from them are a magnificent gold filigree sword-pommel and some other items with animal ornament. The finds from the seventh century are more numerous, and increase in succeeding centuries. Swedish forms are dominant, though in the seventh and eighth centuries there are many graves with west Finnish grave goods; these are particularly numerous in the large Kvarnbacken cemetery in Saltvik parish, the complete excavation yielding 140 monuments. The women's graves included west Finnish equal-armed and crayfish brooches, and other ornaments are also mainland types. The same is true of the weapons, which include some Finnish types lacking in Sweden, like the 'angos'.

The appearance of these mounds (*ättehög*) on Åland must re-present a new settlement and a new culture, and it is clear that immigrants had come from both west and east. The former had evidently moved there from central Sweden, probably round Lake Mälaren, where the grave mounds and much of the grave furniture find their closest parallels. The latter certainly came from the south-western part of Finland proper. There is not enough material to estimate the relative proportions of these two groups.

The new arrivals apparently settled first in the eastern part of the main island, on the fertile clay plain, and seem to have been agriculturalists from the beginning. At the same time one can scarcely overestimate the importance of fishing, fowling, seal hunting and seafaring for them, and it has even been suggested that the settlement was a deliberate colonization to exploit the economic possibilities of organized mass seal hunting. It is clear that the sea was a natural source of wealth, as the forest was in inland parts of Finland. As far as one can see, the settlement expanded only very slowly and certainly did not take over the whole island at once.

The settlement and its culture show no sudden changes during the Viking period though finds take on a more exclusively Swed-ish complexion. Dominant types are Scandinavian oval tortoise brooches, equal-armed brooches, armrings with wavy ornament and Thor's-hammer rings. Typically Swedish also are the 'chess-men' or gaming pieces of bone, stone or horn, and the long combs made of triple bone plates. As far as one can see at present, Åland during the Viking period was part of central Sweden, and the hoard finds with their Arabic silver coins underline this connection with Birka and central Sweden. These eight finds include 1300 coins, all Arabic. The largest, 800 coins buried in an Oriental bronze bottle, is from Bertby in Saltvik. The coins date from the ninth and tenth centuries, and the oldest find, that from Geta, consists exclusively of coins struck before 825.

These finds have with good reason been regarded as evidence of Åland's participation in Viking ventures to the east, and the silver was the booty, whether robbery loot or mercantile profit. That the silver came straight to Åland and not through any intermediary in Scandinavia is suggested both by the Oriental vase from Bertby, and the early date of Geta where the coins cannot have spent any time in circulation before having been deposited. The special character of these hoards is underlined by their absence from south-west Finland, and there are other features, such as the clay 'claws' which show connections between Åland and eastern Europe. These are hard-baked clay figures in the shape of a human hand or an animal claw. They are often found in Åland graves and presumably had magic significance. They are unknown from the rest of the Baltic (with the exception of one fragment from Södermanland in Sweden) but are frequent in the so-called Merian cemeteries of central Russia which include numerous Swedish Viking objects and are sometimes connected with wandering Swedes. These graves are common on the upper Volga and the Oka. As the claws appear in Åland before the Viking period, and in Russia only in the Viking period, they may well have originated in Åland.

The mounds in Åland would seem to have gone out of use about AD 1000 as no later objects have been found in the graves. It would seem from the situation of the rectangular stone-edged mounds in the cemeteries that they are the latest graves in them; they were evidently inhumations made under Christian influence. They are few in number, and soon after this, people began to bury the dead in consecrated ground round the first Christian churches, abandoning the old mounds. The medieval stone

Plate 51

churches of Åland were preceded by small wooden churches afterwards included in the stone building or abandoned; there are references to old church sites which show this.

Absence of heathen burial after AD 1000 suggests that Åland was christianized at the beginning of the eleventh century. It has been urged on the other hand that it shows a depopulation by emigration, and that a new population, also from Sweden, came to Åland during the historic period. This is very unlikely. The house sites from the prehistoric period into the Middle Ages are of the same type and indicate a continuous culture. The absence of graves is more plausibly explained by the advent of Christ-ianity, for we know that the Church was active in the Baltic at the time.

KARELIA

A settled Iron Age population is not found before the transition to the Viking period at the end of the eighth century in the for-merly Finnish (now Russian) parts of Karelia, the coast west and north of Lake Ladoga. The find from Riekkala already described (p. 89) certainly is much earlier but it is unique and is an isolated grave not a cemetery. All the Iron Age finds from the region before the Viking period are stray finds: oval strike-a-lights and a few axes and spearheads, which show only that people from different places journeyed here, from west Finland, Estonia, and central and eastern Russia.

The earliest real cemetery is a cairn of west Finnish type con-taining cremations and west Finnish artifacts, on the west shore of Lake Ladoga in Sakkola. The earliest traces of peasant culture in Karelia are attributable to immigrants from western Finland, as the centuries-long expansion there reached the shore of Ladoga. It is symptomatic that this happened on the threshold of the Viking period when the trade routes through Russia opened, and altered the economic situation of the Gulf of Finland. The new economic activity is clearly reflected in the Viking age finds from the Ladoga region.

Only a few cemeteries of the Viking period have been found, and they are cremations under a level surface or cairns of turf and stone. The grave goods are mainly west Finnish in type, to a lesser extent Scandinavian or Finno-Ugric (here meaning ob-jects typical of the Finno-Ugrian regions in central and northern Russia). These cemeteries are clearly relics of immigration from western Finland though they do not enable us to specify from what part of it the settlers came, as the objects are types common to the whole of western Finland. Nor can we establish by what route they came, though scattered finds from Tavastia and Savo suggest connections across the intervening lake plateau.

The Scandinavian objects in the finds seem to come from the south, from the so-called Viking colonies in north Russia. The gold armring from Metsäpirtti, the only golden object from Fin-land's later Iron Age, is particularly interesting. It is a broad open ring tapered at the ends and decorated on the upper surface with cross ridges and lines of dots. It may be an ornament, but is most probably a medium of exchange. No comparable gold rings are known, but similar rings of silver (often broken) are quite common in hoards of the Viking period in Gotland, and they also occur elsewhere in Scandinavia. A fragment of a silver ring was found in the great hoard in Nousiainen (p. 117). Some have assumed that the ring derives from a Viking centre in Rus-sia, and even attributed it to a Viking ruler dominating the district. It may be an offering. But the possibility that it came direct from Sweden through the ever-increasing trade must be allowed. It should be noted that filigree-ornamented embossed gold pendants have been found in north-east Estonia; these cer-tainly came from Sweden and scarcely got to Estonia via the Viking colonies. The find dates from the beginning of the tenth century and is perhaps somewhat older than the ring from Kare-lia, but it shows that western gold objects travelled the whole

Plate 58

length of the usual trade route to the eastern parts of the Gulf of Finland, which may support the view that the ring from Karelia is also of western provenance.

Even if we assume that people from western Finland settled western Karelia, that is not the whole story of how the Iron Age culture of Karelia began. A culture area also flourished on the south-east shores of Lake Ladoga, evidently locals who only now began to use metals and thus provide us with archaeological evidence. The river banks from the Volchov to the Svir are rich in cemeteries of the Viking period and after, with mounds known as *kurgans*. The grave goods include many Scandinavian forms and the mounds have often been interpreted as relics of Swedish Viking colonization. On the other hand they also include many objects of local Finno-Ugric type, and the original population was certainly Finno-Ugrian. Scandinavian types are most common in the richer graves, which may be those of merchants and chieftains.

North of the Svir, near the former frontier, some *kurgans* have been excavated in which the dead were buried unburnt in a simple plank frame placed on the original ground surface. This wooden enclosure does not occur in mounds further south, but there are parallels west of Ladoga, where inhumations of the crusading period (1050–1300) sometimes have a log or plank frame in the bottom of the grave. The grave mounds north of Svir are older than these but there is evidently some connection, seen also in the finds from them.

These similarities have led to the view that a unified population lived round Lake Ladoga; it is quite possible that the west and north shores had indigenous inhabitants who lacked metal and have left no traces. Influenced from different quarters, these subsequently developed along different lines. The people of the south-east and east coast were strongly influenced by the Vikings, acquired their own culture and were, or with time became, what we have come to know as the Veps. Karelian culture on the other hand was formed by the people of the west and north coasts and perhaps settlers from western Finland, under strong influence from Gotland and Novgorod. In other words it is only at the end of the Viking period that one can distinguish different tribes around Lake Ladoga. The increase in trade and cultural contact typical of the Viking period drew these regions into the general development, though in different ways and with different consequences.

The area round Käkisalmi (Kexholm) on the western side of Ladoga is the heart of the Karelian culture of the crusading period, and a number of large and well-furnished cemeteries have been excavated here. The inhabited area north of Ladoga is mainly recognizable by its forts, but some graves have been found, the easternmost near Sortavala.

The graves are inhumation burials, with few exceptions orientated north/south. Sometimes there is a timber framework in the bottom of the grave, in which the dead man was laid fully clad and with lavish grave goods. Here as in western Finland inhumation burial gradually replaced cremation, which was the most usual rite during the Viking period. Cemeteries of the crusading period often preserved features of the older cremation burials, and sometimes one cremation burial is found in a cemetery which otherwise only includes inhumations. An arrangement of stones either immediately on top of or somewhat above an unburnt body is also a link with the older cremation rites. On the other hand we also find graves completely without grave goods in the same cemetery as very well-furnished graves, and occurring in such numbers that one can only assume that they represent a change to Christian burial customs, though the old burial-place was not at first abandoned. These unfurnished graves are usually orientated west/east.

The finds include many types specifically Karelian, only rarely found outside the region. Oval tortoise-brooches used as shoulder brooches, and large horseshoe-shaped brooches of thin

Fig. 29
Plate 59

137

Fig. 29 Ornaments of woman's dress, Karelia (AD 1050–1300). Length of oval shoulder brooches about 8 cm.

embossed silver decorated with Karelian plant ornament are characteristic, as are finely plaited sausage-shaped hair ornaments of silver wire, ornamented chains with cross-shaped, pierced chain-holders, bronze tubes and bronze beads threaded on a leather thong fastened to a bronze or iron chain.

In the graves were found many round Gotland silver brooches with a variety of ornamentation, certainly imported, but so common that they may be regarded as typical of Karelian folk costume. A number of eastern Finno-Ugric ornaments also occur, particularly bird-shaped pendants with small bells attached. Very rarely, and only in the hoards, some Slavonic ornaments occur, such as rings for the temples or ears.

Karelian plant ornament of the acanthus type, is a mixed style which blends Byzantine features of plant and palmetto with western geometric styles. Its origin has been sought in Novgorod,

Plate 60

but though that might explain the Byzantine features the ornament itself cannot be so explained in its entirety, as no object in this style has ever been found in the city. The frequency with which it occurs in Karelia suggests that it originated or was carried out there. Apart from the large silver horseshoe brooches it occurs on ordinary objects such as knife handles and sheaths, belt mounts and so on. It is true that it required skilled craftsmen for its execution, but why should one not credit Karelia with such?

Christian objects occur in both men's and women's graves, and come both from western and eastern sources. To the GreekOrthodox church belong two round silver embossed pendants, one showing the Virgin Mary in prayer, the other decorated with a cross. A small ringbrooch with the inscription *AVE MARIA GT* is western. A number of pendant crosses of silver or bronze are of a type widely distributed in both east and west, and a silver chain with animalhead endsockets, certainly of Scandinavian workmanship, carries some RussianByzantine crosses in a silver ring. In this case, as in ornament and cultural contacts, Karelia, lying between two great trading powers and two Churches, was subject to influence from east and west.

Plate 61

Plate 63

Weapons are relatively rare, but some splendid swords with bronze or silverinlaid grips do occur, as well as various spearheads. Traces of armour both ringmail and iron plate survive, the oldest of their kind found in Finland.

The graves are more richly provided with household implements and tools than in western Finland. Iron pans, bronze cauldrons and dishes, sickles and scythes, spades, hammers, planes and knives all occur. The axes with long caliclelike sockets are characteristic; needles, awls, scissors and distaffs are found in women's graves. The pottery is wheelturned and flatbottomed, often decorated with wavy lines.

More than twenty prehistoric forts exist in Karelia, closest together along the north shore of Ladoga, and finds from them show that at least some were in use during both the Viking and crusading periods. The best known of these is Tiuri which is situated on what used to be an island in the river Vuoksi connecting Lake Saimaa with Ladoga. This was a fortified trading-place, a 'town'. It was originally, before the level of the Vuoksi was lowered last century, surrounded by the river and therefore well protected, the ramparts of the fort descending straight into the water. As a result of the lowering operation the river's eastern channel dried up, uniting the island to the shore, whilst the western channel was cleared and bridged. The highest point is now 7 metres above water-level, and the walled area is 60 metres wide and 230 metres long. The width of the walls is 4 – 5 metres, their height measured from outside 1.7 metres.

Tiuri is mentioned in Russian chronicles of the beginning of the fifteenth century as *Tiverski prigorod*. We do not know when this 'suburb' *(prigorod)* of Novgorod was founded, but a date in the crusading period seems likely, and a silver hoard found in the fort dates from that time. Nor do we know whether it was originally a place of refuge or was from the beginning a fortified trading-place as its situation suggests.

Graves and cemeteries with Karelian material, either some or all of the objects in which are of exclusively Karelian type, have been found outside the focal district mentioned above; the culture expanded both west and south. It colours the area round Mikkeli in the crusading period, stretches as far as eastern Tavastia and even leaves some traces in Ingria in north Russia. The biggest and richest of the cemeteries is at Tuukkala near Mikkeli in Savo. It contains about fifty graves, mainly inhumation burials orientated west/east or south-west/north-east. The grave goods are entirely Karelian, though the combinations vary slightly. Among the finds are many horseshoe-shaped and round silver brooches; the latter included the only object found in Finland with a runic incription, the name *Botvi* of a Gotland woman inscribed on the inside. The cemetery in Tuukkala was for long regarded as evidence of colonization from Karelia, but the picture changed with the discovery of Viking Age cemeteries in the same parish. These are related to the common west Finnish expansion eastwards and the Karelian complexion of the later cemetery at Tuukkala must then be attributed simply to cultural borrowing, as the west Finnish settlers came into close contact, perhaps for economic reasons, with the Ladoga Karelian culture, and adopted much of its material. One must also remember that west Finnish material from the end of the twelfth and the thirteenth century (Tuukkala and the Karelian finds in Tavastia are from so late a date) is not well enough known to permit satisfactory comparison.

The development of Iron Age culture in Karelia is apparently related to the increasing eastern trade and the economic changes it involved. When in the eleventh century the routes to the Arab world were severed, and ventures to the east ceased, Sweden's and particularly Gotland's economic activity seems to have concentrated on the Baltic, particularly its eastern part. The new centre was Novgorod which soon became very important to the merchants of Gotland, who even had their own guild there. Novgorod gradually extended its influence to Karelia, and already by the twelfth century men of Novgorod and Karelia were said have formed an alliance. Influences from Gotland on the one hand and Novgorod on the other stimulated developments in Karelia, and its prosperity during the crusading period is due to both.

At the time when the area around Käkisalmi on the west side of Ladoga began to be distinguishable as a unified culture, the water route from Viipuri (Viborg) via Vuoksi to Käkisalmi was at the peak of its importance. Tiuri and Käkisalmi, perhaps the later Viipuri as well, were important stages on the trade route. Finds dating from before this period are not known from these districts. Indeed only one small find of the crusading period is known from Viipuri, from a place which later became a Christian churchyard, though we cannot exclude the possibility that it was already a trading centre at this date. It is difficult to believe that the place to which Tyrgils Knutsson, a shrewd and success-ful leader of Swedish expansion eastwards, took his expedition in 1293, and where he built Viipuri castle as Sweden's eastern fortress against Novgorod, was entirely uninhabited.

We have evidence of the presence of western merchants on this Vuoksi route in a hoard from Heinjoki which mainly con-sists of Frisian coins and is attributed to a Frisian merchant visi-ting Karelia because of its combination of coin types. The find, from about AD 1070, is the oldest definite sign of direct Frisian activity in Finland. Many objects, some already mentioned, attest the importance of Gotland trade. To it are attributable the weapons found in Karelia.

A hoard from the end of the eleventh century from Rautu has been connected with the other route to the east, the Neva. Nov-gorod's link with the north was naturally the river Volchov which flows into Lake Ladoga. Thence the route went to the inhabited parts of Karelia and along the Neva and across the Gulf of Finland to Gotland. The Novgorod influence in Karelia is obvious, though it is not easy to produce unambiguous mate-rial proof. There can be no doubt that the Greek Orthodox Christian objects found in Karelia came through Novgorod, and we have historical sources to support this. For instance, Prince Jaroslav of Novgorod, Vsevolod's son, had a number of Karelians baptized in 1227. Most of the Christian objects came from richly furnished graves with the heathen north/south orien-tation, and one must make the same reservation about these graves as about the similar ones in west Finland; they are not indisput-able evidence that those buried there were Christians. For, as was pointed out as early as 1880 by a knowledgeable student of the crusading period in Karelia, the cross was a symbol which could have been held sacred either by the deceased or by those who survived him.

Silver is plentiful in finds of the crusading period and shows the prosperity of the Karelians, based no doubt on fur-trading; the Karelians bought furs up in north Finland and Lapland (p. 147), and then delivered the goods to Novgorod. Both written and archaeological sources testify to this trade or forced taxation of the Lapps. The demand for furs was evidently unlimited, and a fifteenth-century source relates that the people of Novgorod on one occasion took fifty thousand squirrel skins and many sables as tribute from their neighbours to the north-east; the quantities could be truly enormous.

In a trade treaty of 1342 between Novgorod and German merchants, delivery from that centre of pure genuine wax is mentioned. Novgorod was only an intermediary and it has been suggested that Karelia was one of the regions in which the wax was purchased; also a find (not from Karelia but from the valley of the river Vaga in north Russia) has been connected with the wax trade. It is a bronze balance, four weights and two fragments of wax, evidently a merchant's store of his purchases. But where did the merchant come from? Was he from Novgorod or, as is more probable, from the Ladoga area? We cannot tell, and in any case the find is scarcely evidence of the export of wax from Karelia.

The material objects from Karelia in the crusading period are very different from those found in western Finland, but we must remember that they are from later graves, and some of the objects we regard as particularly Karelian may well have been known in western Finland as well. A hint of this is to be seen in the sheath with Karelian plant ornament found in excavations in the town of Turku.

Chapter VIII

Iron Age relics in North Finland and Lapland

RIGHT UP TO THE END of the prehistoric period it was, as we have seen, only a small part of Finland that was permanently inhabited. The greater part of the country was an uninhabited expanse offering excellent hunting and trapping and thus providing the basis for the trade of the settlements and their wealth. How far Lapps or other aborigines existed outside the settlements archaeology can only partially determine.

It is scarcely an exaggeration to say that all the inhabited parts of Finland have had their own *eräkausi,* or fur-trading period. There is no doubt that hunting was decisive for the new settlements, even if agriculture was practised and helped to make existence more secure. Agriculture could not have assured the prosperity revealed by the finds; it was in the forest that the key to riches lay. This appears also from the details in early historical sources about the carefully delimited areas for the chase which belonged to particular settlements.

Objects found outside inhabited areas are to be regarded as traces of hunting expeditions, and the few burials represent merely temporary habitation. The spread of the oval strike-a-lights already mentioned shows how far hunting expeditions extended. It was nevertheless not until the late Iron Age that north Finland and Lapland seem to have attracted the interest of enterprising people from all quarters; and in the last centuries of the Iron Age, signs of this increasing interest multiply.

Stray finds from the area between the settled regions of the south and Lapland may show the routes taken, but are so sparse that firm conclusions are scarcely justifiable. Finds seem more concentrated in central Ostrobothnia and on the north Ostrobothnian coast, but they occur in north Tavastia, Savo and Karelia as well. We know from historical sources that Lapps

lived in Olonets at the end of the prehistoric period, and in Savo
and Karelia into the sixteenth century, but neither their dwelling-sites nor burial places are known. The reason is that the
Lapps had little metal and used bone, horn and wood right up
to our own day; and these materials do not survive long. The
Lapps did however get some metal from people to the south,
partly on their own southward wanderings but mainly from
contacts with fur buyers and other enterprising men who came
north. The wealth of furs certainly lured not only buyers but also hunters and tax leviers from the south, and the hoards from
north Finland reflect this activity which is also seen in some
offerings found in Swedish Lapland.

These offerings, about ten in all, distinguish themselves by the
many metal objects and coins from the period AD 1000–1300
which they contain, as well as the reindeer bone and horn common to all Lapp sacrificial sites. The most important are Rautas-
jaure in Jukkasjärvi, Unna Saiva and Saivo in Gällivare and
Gråträsk in Piteå. The metal objects, though numerous, are insignificant and often fragmentary. Some are cast in bronze with
a large tin content and are evidently of Lapp manufacture. The
remaining material is very varied: west Finnish, Karelian, Finno-Ugric (*i.e.* like the Russian Finno-Ugric cemetery material),
east Baltic, Norwegian, etc. There is little south Swedish material, and what there is from Gotland consists of forms which are
also common in western Finland.

The west Finnish contribution is from the eleventh century;
it includes some very characteristic forms: round west Finnish
brooches, equal-armed brooches with knobs, horseshoe brooches, a bear-tooth amulet of bronze and so on. Probably some of
the Gotland material also came through Finland. Four copies of
Arabic coins, found at Gråträsk, seem to have been made in
Finland or in the eastern Baltic. They can be dated to about 1015.
German and Anglo-Saxon types of coins are also common in
Finland.

The Karelian element is less strong and seems to be later, dat- ing from the twelfth and thirteenth centuries. The east Baltic objects and those from Ingria, as well as some of the Finno- Ugric ones, also probably come immediately from Karelia, though the latter might equally well have reached the north by a route east of Lake Ladoga.

Some of the objects from these offerings form a group on their own; they belong to those spread all over northern Europe during the Hanseatic period. In part at least they probably came from Norway, for the finds are very rich in Norwegian coins, and these dominate the picture in the twelfth century, evidently in conse- quence of a change in the pattern of trade, in which there was now an increasing Norwegian emphasis.

It seems beyond doubt that at least some of the west Finnish material was brought by visitors from south-west Finland, and the west Finnish objects from north Norwegian finds at this date support this. Some of these are also much earlier, at least as early as the tenth century. Egil's saga tells of strife between Norsemen, Kvens (western Finns) and Karelians for the overlordship of Lapland. Lapp offerings in Sweden suggest that conditions were the same at the end of the Iron Age as in the early Middle Ages.

With the exception of a small one from Ukonsaari in Inari, there are no similar finds from Finland. Arthur Evans excavated there on an expedition in the eighteen-seventies finding a cave full of reindeer bones whose entrance was surrounded by a semi- circle of reindeer antlers. The only find was a silver filigree ear- ring of east Russian type. Stray finds alone are known from Fin- nish Lapland throughout the Viking period and later. In the ninth and tenth centuries there are signs of north Scandinavian activity; Scandinavian oval brooches and other objects were found in the latitude of Oulu. They mark a connection, perhaps a trade route, which ran across Finland to the White Sea, or else turned south to south-east Finland as a certain sixteenth-century description of a Karelian trade route might imply. The activity was probably mainly Norwegian, as is shown by some Norwegian finds even further north. West Finnish and Karelian objects occur later. The finds which most illuminate the eleventh and twelfth centuries are the hoards, three from Kuusamo, one from Salla and one from Ylitornio (Övertorneä). A description survives of a find (now lost) from Kemijärvi and some stray finds of silver ornaments.

One of the Kuusamo finds consists exclusively of silver coins, over four hundred in number, and mainly German. The find from Salla includes both coins and silver ornaments and scales with weights. The other hoards are of silver ornaments, particularly neck- and armrings, brooches and pendants. They are widely distributed types, but no exact parallels can be cited, and views about their provenance are varied. Some have concluded that they were made specially for the Lapp trade, probably in Novgorod, whilst more recent investigations suggest Karelian manufacture.

Plate 64

These finds too have been explained as sacrificial offerings, particularly because of the associated place-names. One of the Kuusamo finds is at a place called Ukonlahti at the foot of mount Ukonvaara; *Ukko* is the name of the Finnish sky-god. Another of the Kuusamo finds is near Lake Pyhäjärvi (Holy Lake) and the lost hoard from Kemijärvi was on a hill called Termusvaara whose name has been derived from the Lapp thunder-god Tiermes. No reindeer antlers, characteristic of Lapp sacrifical rites, have been found at any of these places; it is therefore difficult to interpret the finds as offerings by Lapps, and it is unlikely that they are offerings by hunters or fur buyers from the south. They are probably simply treasure buried by Lapps or, as it might seem from the scales and weights at Salla, by merchants from the south.

All these hoards are from between AD 1050 and 1150. A silver hoard from the mouth of the river Varzuga on the Kola peninsula is earlier, being at the latest from the Viking period. It consists of a neckring with hook and loop ends and an armring, both of silver. At this date it is most likely to have come from the region south-east of Ladoga. The armring is Scandinavian, but the neckring is Permian.

This find takes us to the White Sea coast, the Biarmaland of the sagas. The name occurs for the first time (about 870) in Alfred's translation of Orosius, where an account by the Norwegian Ottar of a voyage north and east from Halogaland is inserted. His voyage took him to a region, evidently in the White Sea, where he met Biarmians. Another important source is the saga of St Olaf which recounts Tore Hund's voyage with two companions to a trading place of the Biarmians on the river Vinu (Dvina) in AD 1026. The account includes the well-known story of the destruction and plundering of the Biarmians' idol of the god Jomali. Though the story is a mixture of fact and fiction the journey itself and its destination may be taken as being authentic.

Modern Finnish research regards Biarmaland as a name for the regions surrounding the White Sea, sometimes restricted to the mouth of the Dvina, sometimes in a very extended sense; 'Biarmia was probably a vague zone between Finnmark, the White Sea, Lake Onega and Ladoga.' (A. M. Tallgren) There are no archaeological finds in sites from this region in the later Iron Age, and it was doubtless inhabited only by half-nomadic hunters, Lapps, Syryenians and Samoyeds.

During the Viking period the White Sea regions evidently belonged to the sphere of interest of the south-east Ladoga settlement. This is suggested by the find from the Varzuga and by the fact that signs of permanent habitation such as graves have been found from the north and north-east shores of Lake Onega at the end of the Viking period. Furthermore a silver hoard with Arab coins has been found at Petrozavodsk at the mouth of the Neglinka. The graves and their furnishings are the same as in the region south-east of Ladoga. Connections between the north end of Lake Onega and the White Sea were good, and the graves reflect activity from Ladoga in that direction.

One need not be surprised by the lack of finds from the White Sea coast even at the mouth of the Dvina. The trading posts situated there were very temporary markets where seller and buyer met at agreed times, leaving few signs above ground and to be found only by a lucky chance.

It is generally held nowadays that the word *biarm* is a description of a calling; that of a forest-ranging hunter who undertook long hunting expeditions. During the Viking period they were at home in the region south-east of Ladoga; later, when settlement west and north of Ladoga had consolidated, they may have come from there as well. A sixteenth-century description of routes from Karelia to Oulu in north Finland and to the White Sea might suggest this. The White Sea offered economic possibilities other than fur hunting and trading. Historical sources tell us that salt boiling was carried on there as early as 1137, and pearl fishing in the east Karelian rivers and wax collecting also took place.

CHAPTER IX

Settlement and Society in the Iron Age

THE DEVELOPMENT of Finland during the prehistoric period was conditioned by its situation between east and west. Its overland contacts with the east led, particularly in the earliest stages, to valuable cultural influence and many immigrants. During the Stone Age it formed part of the widespread combed-ware culture but even then there are traces of contacts across the sea with the west. The arrival of the boat-axe culture divided the country into two provinces; the Kiukais culture at the end of the Stone Age shows one culture embracing the east and west sides of the Gulf of Bothnia and the northern Baltic; and in the Bronze Age the coastal regions were directly linked to the Scandinavian world.

We cannot follow these developments of long ago as an integrated whole, at least not with our present-day resources. During the Iron Age the country was made up of four different settled areas, all to some extent peasant ones, whose Iron Ages began and ended at different times and whose type objects varied greatly. Only in the south-west do we get a picture of a continuous development from the beginning of our era into historic times and down to the present day as immigrants from the south settled and expanded slowly eastwards. It was this settlement which consolidated Finnish society, and from that time on we can follow its development step by step. It is thus scarcely an exaggeration to say that the characteristics of Finnish society were determined by its western contacts as these enriched the east Baltic foundation which the immigrants brought with them. Finland's position on the coast was decisive.

The most important element in the genesis of the Finnish people was the immigration from south of the Gulf of Finland, but from the very beginning other factors were present. The mate-

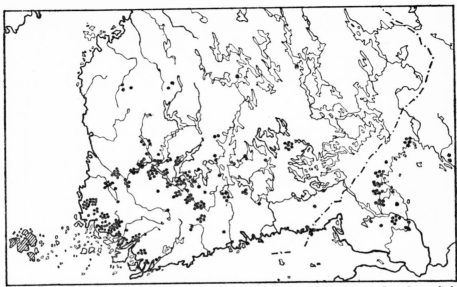

Fig. 30   Distribution of cemeteries in Finland at the end of the prehistoric period. Hatching denotes high-density over-all spread

rial shows that people from the south coast of the Baltic, in the area of the Vistula, and from the west of the Baltic, in Scandinavia, played their part. How important it was we do not know; it is clear for example that there were immigrations from Sweden, but not continuous and probably never very large. The role of the aboriginal inhabitants remains vague, as it was not shown by the use of metal which came in with the immigrants of the first centuries. We have attempted to give an account of this process in the earlier chapters and it is unnecessary to repeat it here. Let us rather glance at conditions immediately prior to the historic period.

Our map shows the distribution of cemeteries and grave finds *Fig. 30* from the end of the prehistoric period and gives some idea of the

distribution of the people. It shows very clearly how little of Finland was inhabited by a settled population. North of a line from
the lower reaches of the Kokemäki to Ikaalinen and through
Tampere and Mikkeli to the north coast of Lake Ladoga there
are few traces of habitation, and there are large uninhabited areas
south of it. Big forests separated inhabited Finland proper from
the inhabited regions in Tavastia's lake district; both Uusimaa
and western Karelia were to a large extent uninhabited; and
particularly in eastern Tavastia and Savo, settlements were surrounded by wilderness. If the islands off Finland proper were
already inhabited by Sweden, the Christian community there
left no archaeological evidence. The same may have been true
of Uusimaa, but it is generally supposed that deliberate colonization there did not begin until the historic period.

Even if one can establish small local differences for geographical reasons, the material culture of the south-west, and probably
its culture as a whole, was very homogeneous. Naturally enough,
the coastal population had closer contacts with other countries
than that of Tavastia, and was more rapidly affected by changes
of fashion. But the cemeteries and forts are in general identical.
Offering stones are found over the whole area, and the fact that
there are more of them inland is not so much because they were
more characteristic of those districts, as because they were further
from the bishop's palace in Turku; the Church's action against
heathenism was naturally more effective nearer home.

In spite of this homogeneity, Finland was not an administrative, much less a political unit during this period. There were
villages in the central area, perhaps also larger units, and at the
end of the prehistoric period certain tribal groups emerge. The
forts point to social co-operation in face of the threat of danger,
and must have belonged to relatively large units, tribes, resulting
from the common economic and other interests and common
fate of neighbours. In Sweden a distinction was made between
Fii ns and Finland (Finland proper), and Tavastians and Ta-

vastia (Häme). The sixteenth-century contention that Tavastia once stretched from sea to sea (both salt) must imply an organer unity between settlements round the Kokemäki river valley (Ala-Satakunta) and southern Tavastia.

It was only in the historic period that Finland became an administrative and political unit, but the conditions for the establishment of an Österland (an old Swedish name for Finland) and a later Finland were to be found in the common cultural inheritance of the people. There was opposition between the inhabitants of Tavastia and those of Karelia, and Russian sources report repeated clashes between them in the early historic period; in Lapland the interests of Karelians and western Finns were opposed. The country was eventually unified by foreign conquest which made it part of the kingdom of Sweden.

Finnish society has already been characterized as a peasant society, yet the grave finds do show some divisions of social class. The rich, splendidly equipped graves are worthy of chieftains, and it seems natural that a wealthy landowner should be buried with more pomp than less important members of the family, not to mention the servants. The graves devoid of goods in the late inhumation cemeteries, if they are not Christian, are perhaps those of slaves. Archaeology can tell us nothing certain of this class, but we know that slavery was common in Viking society and that slaves were exported to the markets of the east. To judge from folk poetry, slavery also existed in Finland.

The graves rich in weapons can only be called chieftains' graves with some reservations. It depends whether this term is used to describe a leader chosen by the people, or the head of a powerful clan, or some other rich and powerful man. For war or defence, leaders must have been appointed, but we do not know on what basis. The words *ruhtinas* (prince) and *kun-ingas* (king) were in use, but their precise meaning can scarcely be established. It seems that all free men had weapons, so that graves with weapons are no evidence of a military caste.

The population was mainly confined to the coasts and river banks along which it had spread. Waterways are natural routes, but there were also tracks on land, for horses and men if not for wheeled vehicles, uniting the valleys of Finland proper with each other, and one such has been found between Uusikaupunki and the bend of the Kokemäki river. The many finds of bits and harness in the graves show the extent to which horses were used.

No towns of the prehistoric period are known, and only one established market place, Tiuri in Karelia, but they must have existed. The 'towns' whose scarcely identifiable names occur in early sources cannot be located, and no certain traces of them have been found. The finds suggest that important markets must have been situated near the mouth of the Aura, close to or actually within modern Turku; near the Männäinen near Uusikaupunki in northern Finland proper; at Halikko bay in the south; and in Kokemäki near the great bend of the river. Two place-names in the Novgorod chronicle's account in the year 1188 of prisoners taken by the Varangians (Vikings) and Germans from Gotland have been interpreted as Koroinen and 'new Turku' pointing to the mouth of the Aura. As long as the sites remain undiscovered their age and importance must be an open question.

The most important factor in eleventh-century trade was Gotland, whose contacts covered the whole Baltic and reached as far as Novgorod. Novgorod's trade with Finland was mainly concentrated on Karelia, but also extended to west Finland, and the Novgorod source already cited mentions not only Varangians (Swedes from Sweden?) but also Germans and men of Novgorod as meeting in Turku. How far Finnish peasants undertook foreign voyages at this period is uncertain, but contact with the west coast of the Gulf of Bothnia was certainly maintained as Finnish objects from Birka show.

Trade in weapons has left clear traces, and seems to have been carried on mainly by Gotland. This is supported not only by archaeological evidence but by a papal bull of 1229 forbidding

Gotlanders to sell arms to the heathen who threatened the Finnish Church. The import of metals, whether iron, bronze or silver, is always archaeologically better recorded than are organic materials such as salt, spices and cloth. The inhabitants of the Kokemäki valley had excellent hunting opportunities in the north after the depopulation of south Ostrobothnia in the Viking period, and the Tavastians lived near an extensive region of wilderness where fur-bearing animals abounded; it is easy to see whence they got their wealth. It is harder to understand the prosperity of Finland proper, where an expanding population lacked such opportunities. If agriculture produced an exportable surplus of flour and butter in the south, this cannot have been the case in the north where the poor stony soil can never have done so. It has already been suggested that trade, both foreign and internal, must have been important to the people near Uusikaupunki. There are many finds from this region and they show a close connection with Birka. The trade-route to the Kokemäki valley probably left the coast at this point, as the lower reaches of the Kokemäki river were difficult or impossible to navigate, and many centuries later peasants from Tavastia undertook long journeys to trade in Uusikaupunki. Other resources may have been seal hunting and fishing; and the possibility should be born in mind too, that it was the men of this region who were the Kvens who travelled to Lapland, and are described in Scandinavian saga accounts of the struggle for its riches. If so they travelled by sea, along the Gulf of Bothnia, to trade or exact tribute. This would explain the west Finnish objects in the Lapp sacrificial offerings in Swedish Lapland.

These Lapland expeditions in folklore and saga are tinged with romance and heroism. But the real Finnish culture had its origin in the farms, slowly but surely achieving independence and originality, adopting western features but adapting them to a substantial part of the national culture. This development did not create a nation in the political or administrative sense until the

Swedish conquest in the eleven-fifties joined western Finland to the neighbouring kingdom and in the following century extended its control to Tavastia and subsequently to Karelia; but it had created the conditions and laid the foundations for the development of a national unit, and the eventual emergence, after many centuries and many reversals, of an independent Finnish nation and Finnish state.

Select Bibliography

There is no scholarly presentation in English of Finland's pre-history as a whole. A recent work is the author's *Suomen esihistoria* (Finnish), 1961, and *Finlands förhistoria* (Swedish), 1964. The most important archaeological publications are in the series of the Finnish Archaeological Society (*Suomen Muinaismuistoyh-distys*), *Suomen Museo, Finskt Museum, Suomen Muinaismuistoyh-distyksen Aikakauskirja* and *Eurasia Septentrionalis Antiqua*. The ar-ticles in the two first-mentioned yearbooks have summaries in German, the *Aikakauskirja* covers generally larger works in Ger-man or English and *Eurasia* deals mainly with East European problems. The journal *Acta Archaeologica*, which is common to the northern countries of Europe is published in Copenhagen in English, German and French. The bibliography given here con-sists mainly of larger works and a lot of recent articles, published in German or with German summaries.

Abbreviations

AA   *Acta Archaeologica*
ESA   *Eurasia Septentrionalis Antiqua*
SMYA   *Suomen Muinaismuistoyhdistyksen Aikakauskirja/Finska Fornminnesföreningens Tidskrift*

General

CLARK, J. G. D., *Prehistoric Europe: The Economic Basis*. Lon-don 1952, rpr. 1965.
TALLGREN, A.M., Geschichte der antiquarischen Forschung in Finnland. *ESA* X, 1936.

The Mesolithic

ÄYRÄPÄÄ, AARNE, Die ältesten steinzeitlichen Funde aus Finnland. *AA* XXI, 1950.

ÄYRÄPÄÄ, AARNE and SAURAMO, MATTI, Von den ältesten Niederlassungen in Finnland. *Sitzungsberichte der Finnischen Akademie der Wissenschaften 1947.* Helsinki 1949.

CLARK, J. G. D., *The Mesolithic Settlement of Northern Europe.* Cambridge 1936.

LUHO, VILLE, Die Askola-Kultur. Die frühmesolithische Steinzeit in Finnland. *SMYA* 57, 1956.

—, Die Komsa-Kultur. *SMYA* 57, 1956.

PÄLSI, SAKARI, Ein steinzeitlicher Moorfund bei Korpilahti im Kirchspiel Antrea, Län Wiborg. *SMYA* 28:2, 1920.

The Neolithic

AILIO, JULIUS, *Die steinzeitlichen Wohnplatzfunde in Finland. I-II.* Helsinki 1909.

ÄYRÄPÄÄ, AARNE, Die Kulturformen der finnischen Steinzeit. *Sitzungsberichte der Finnischen Akademie der Wissenschaften 1937.* Helsinki 1940.

—, Die relative Chronologie der steinzeitlichen Keramik in Finnland. I-II. *AA* I, 1930.

—, Fornfynd från Kyrkslätt och Esbo socknar. *SMYA* 32:1, 1922.

—, Über die Streitaxtkulturen in Russland. Studien über die Verbreitung neolithischer Elemente aus Mitteleuropa nach Osten. *ESA* VIII, 1933.

DREIJER, MATTS, *Ålands äldsta bebyggelse.* Finskt Museum 1940.

EDGREN, TORSTEN, Jäkärlä-gruppen. En västfinsk kulturgrupp under yngre stenåldern. *SMYA* 64, 1966.

LAITAKARI, AARNE, Die Schaftlochäxte der Steinzeit von geologisch- petro-graphischem Standpunkt. *SMYA* 37:1, 1928.

LUHO, VILLE, Über steinzeitliche Winterkehrsmittel in Finnland. *AA* XIX, 1948.

—, *Suomen kivikauden pääpiirteet.* Helsinki 1948.

MEINANDER, C. F., Die Kiukaiskultur. *SMYA* 53, 1954.
NORDMAN, C. A., *Die steinzeitlichen Tierskulpturen Finnlands.*
Ipek 1936/7.
PÄLSI, SAKARI, Riukjärven ja Piiskunsalmen kivikautiset
asuinpaikat Kaukolassa. *SMYA* 28, 1915.

The Bronze Age and the Pre-Roman Age

ÄYRÄPÄÄ, AARNE, Kulturförhållandena i Finland före finnar-
nas invandring. *SMYA* 52:1, 1951.
MEINANDER, C. F., Die Bronzezeit in Finnland. *SMYA* 54,
1954.
TALLGREN, A. M., Suomen skandinaavisesta pronssikaudesta.
Societas Scientiarum Fennica. Årsbok – Vuosikirja XV B: 5, 1937.
—, The Arctic Bronze Age in Europe. *ESA* XI, 1937.

The Iron Age

APPELGREN, HJ., Suomen muinaislinnat. *SMYA* 12, 1891.
APPELGREN-KIVALO, HJ., *Finnische Trachten aus der jüngeren
Eisenzeit.* Helsinki 1907.
CLEVE, NILS, Skelettgravfälten på Kjuloholm i Kjulo. I. Den
yngre folkvandringstiden. *SMYA* 44, 1943.
ERÄ-ESKO, AARNI, Germanic Animal Art of Salin's Style I
in Finland. *SMYA* 63, 1965.
HACKMAN, ALFRED, Das Brandgräberfeld von Pukkila in
Isokyrö. *SMYA* 41, 1938.
—, *Die ältere Eisenzeit in Finnland. I. Die Funde aus den fünf ersten
Jahrhunderten n. Chr.* Helsinki 1905.
KIVIKOSKI, ELLA, *Die Eisenzeit Finnlands.* Plates and text. I-II.
Helsinki 1947, 1951.
—, Die Eisenzeit im Auraflussgebiet, *SMYA* 43, 1939.
—, Husgrunderna i Storhagen, Kulla, Finström. *SMYA* 48:3,
1946.

—, *Kvarnbacken. Ein Gräberfeld der jüngeren Eisenzeit auf Åland.* Helsinki 1963.

—, Skandinavisches in der römischen Eisenzeit Finnlands. *AA* XXV, 1954.

—, Studien zur Birkas Handel im östlichen Ostseegebiet. *AA* VIII, 1937.

—, Zur Herkunft der Karelier und ihrer Kultur. *AA* XV, 1944.

LEPPÄAHO, JORMA, Späteisenzeitliche Waffen aus Finnland. Schwertinschriften und Waffenverzierungen des 9. – 12. Jahrhunderts. *SMYA* 61, 1964.

NORDMAN, C. A., *Anglo-Saxon Coins found in Finland.* Helsinki 1921.

—, Gotländisch oder deutsch – ein Silberkruzifix von Halikko im Eigentlichen Finnland. *AA* XV, 1944.

—, Karelska järnåldersstudier. *SMYA* 34:3, 1924.

—, Schatzfunde und Handelsverbindungen in Finnlands Wikingerzeit. *AA* XIII, 1942.

SALMO, HELMER, Deutsche Münzen in vorgeschichtlichen Funden Finnlands. *SMYA* 47, 1948.

—, Die Waffen der Merowingerzeit in Finnland. *SMYA* 42:1, 1938.

—, Finnische Hufeisenfibeln. *SMYA* 56, 1956.

SCHWINDT, TH., Tietoja Karjalan rautakaudesta. *SMYA* 13, 1893.

TALLGREN, A.M., Biarmia. *ESA* VI, 1931.

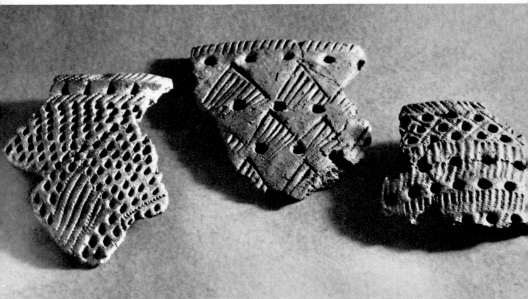

4

5

6

7

8

9

10

11

12   13

14

15

16

17

18

19

20

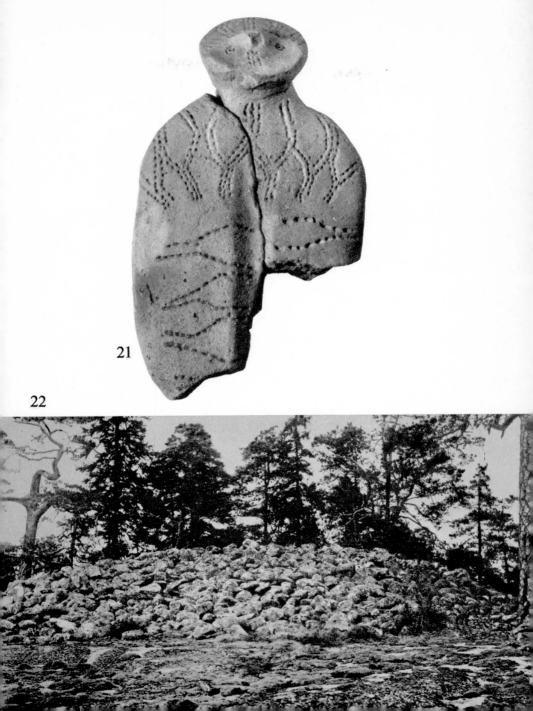

21

22

23

24

25

26

27

28

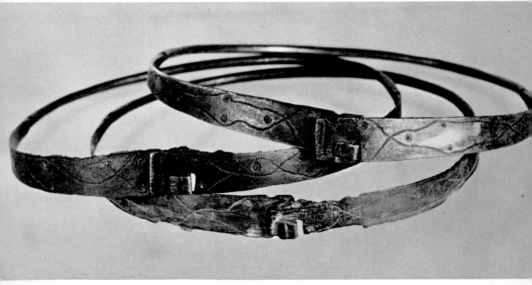

29

30

31

32

33

34

35

36

37

38

39

40

41

42

43

44

45

46

48

49

50

51

52

53

54

55

56

58

59

60   61

62

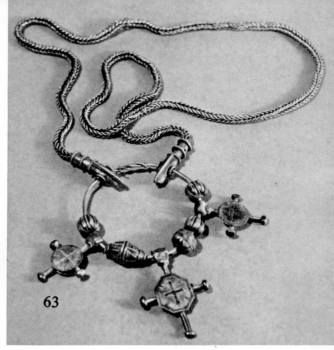

63

64

65

66

Notes on the Plates

1 The Antrea marsh find, from about 7000 BC. Probably the remains of a fisherman's boat and net, which sank in the sea. The floats of the net are nearest the camera, the stone weights in the background. National Museum, Helsinki.

2 Clay vessel of typical combed ware; Pääskylahti, Sääminki, Savo. Height 42 cm. National Museum, Helsinki.

3 Combed ware from Finland. The two pieces on the right are typical, that on the left is eastern pitted ware. National Museum, Helsinki.

4 The Stone Age dwelling-site at Kosinnoniemi, Parikkala, Karelia. Its situation on the sandy beach is characteristic of the combed-ware inland sites.

5 Fireplace of a Stone Age dwelling-site; Pispa, Kokemäki, Satakunta. Diameter about 1 m.

6 Combed ware grave: a stone cist, buried in the ground; Kolmhaara, Honkilahti, Satakunta. The deceased in the cist was covered with red ochre. Length 1.2 m.

7 Slate ring from Kittilä, Lapland. Diameter 7.8 cm. National Museum, Helsinki.

8 Spoon of pinewood *(Pinus cembra)* with bird's-head handle; Pielisjärvi, Karelia. Probably imported from the Ural area in east Russia. Length 13.3 cm. National Museum, Helsinki.

9 Combed-ware grave: a stone cist, buried in the ground; Aisti, Mynämäki, Finland proper. The deceased was covered with red ochre. Length 1.3 m.

10 Detail of bear's-head axe of soapstone; Uura, Paltamo, northern Ostrobothnia. Length 19.1 cm. National Museum, Helsinki.

11 Elk's-head axe (broken) of Karelian green slate; Ravi, Säkkijärvi, Karelia. Length 13.2 cm. National Museum, Helsinki.

12 Stone axe with base modelled as human head; Luelahti, Kiuruvesi, Savo. Length 15.8 cm. National Museum, Helsinki.

13 Sandstone carving with human head; Niskanperä, Rovaniemi, Lapland. Height 5.1 cm. National Museum, Helsinki.

14 Schematized figures of human beings on a rock painting; Juusjärvi, Kirk-konummi, Uusimaa. The painting is executed in red ochre and includes also pictures of fishes, hands and zigzag lines.

15 Clay figure with human head; Nikkarinmäki, Kymi, Uusimaa. Height 5 cm. National Museum, Helsinki.

16 Amber fragment modelled as human face; Koukunniemi, Metsäpirtti, Karelia. Height 5.2 cm. National Museum, Helsinki.

17 Boat axes from western Finland. That on the left is about 20 cm. long. National Museum, Helsinki.

18 Boat-axe burial place on the crest of the rise at Pelttari, Tottijärvi, Sata-kunta.

19 Corded-ware pottery from boat-axe burials in western Finland: Lieto, Lempäälä, Mynämäki. Heights 10.5, 13 and 7.7 cm. National Museum, Helsinki.

20 Neolithic burial on the dwelling-site at Jettböle, Jomala, Åland.

21 Clay figure in human shape from Jettböle, Jomala, Åland. Fragments of about 60 figures of this kind were found on the site. Height 10 cm. National Museum, Helsinki.

22 Bronze age burial cairn; Parainen, Finland proper. Diameter about 15 m., height 2.5 m.

23 Ship-setting of stones placed close together. Late Bronze Age. Grytverks-näset, Sund, Åland. Length 12 m.

24 Burial cist of stone slabs in an excavated Bronze Age cairn; Lähteenmäki, Eura, Satakunta. Length 3 m.

25 Dwelling-site of the late Bronze Age under excavation; Otterböte, Kökar, Åland. The site includes round huts, internal and external fireplaces, heaps of rubbish, remains of a well. The site must be regarded as a seasonal seal-hunters' hamlet.

26 Stone circles in an excavated Bronze Age cairn; Ristniemi, Sauvo, Finland proper. The outermost ring about 11 m. in diameter.

27 Bronze Age clay vessels (for the transport of seal oil?); Otterböte, Kökar, Åland. Height of that on the left 26 cm. Ålands Museum, Mariehamn.

28 Marsh find of three bronze neckrings, probably worn together. End of Bronze Age. Panelia, Kiukainen, Satakunta. Diameters 20, 20.7 and 25 cm. National Museum, Helsinki.

29 Depot of the late Bronze Age; Kuoppala, Kokemäki, Satakunta. The bigger brooch is 25.4 cm. long. National Museum, Helsinki.

30 Cemetery of *tarand* type under excavation; Meeri, Estonia. The burials were situated in the settings of stones and covered with a large cairn. This type of grave was also used in Finland during the Roman Iron Age.

31 Cremation grave of the Roman Iron Age; Kärsämäki, Maaria, Finland proper. The burnt bones and a brooch were put on a slab of sandstone and covered with other slabs.

32 Clay vessel of the Roman Iron age, found in a woman's grave in Kosken-haka, Piikkiö, Finland proper. Length 16.1 cm. National Museum, Helsinki.

33 Gold neckring with animal heads; Nousiainen, Finland Proper. Fourth century AD. 17.1 × 18.2 cm. Statens Historiska Museum, Stockholm.

34 Roman wine ladle, made in Capua, Italy, at the end of the first century AD; Vähäkyrö, south Ostrobothnia. Length 24.1 cm. National Museum, Helsinki.

35 Drinking horn of colourless glass, decorated with blue and milk-white glass threads, found in an inhumation grave in Soukainen, Laitila, Finland proper. Fourth century AD. Provincial-Roman origin. Height 28.5 cm. National Museum, Helsinki.

36 Horseshoe-brooch of bronze, decorated with red and white enamel; Palo, Nousiainen, Finland proper. Fourth century AD. Diameter 9.2 cm. National Museum, Helsinki.

37 East Baltic silver brooch, with ring decoration. Korpolaismäki, Turku. About AD 500. Length 10 cm. Turku Museum.

38 Detail of a bronze knife with a bird's-head handle. Kuulaanmäki, Urjala, Tavastia. Length 10.9 cm. National Museum, Helsinki.

39 Burial mound of the middle Iron Age; Antiala, Tyrväntö, Tavastia. Diameter about 15 m.

40 Cremation cemetery built of stones under level ground; Ristimäki, Kaarina, Finland proper.

41 Weapons in a cremation burial at Ristimäki, Kaarina, Finland proper. Eighth century AD.

42 Sword with bronze hilt, decorated with animal ornaments; Ristimäki, Kaarina, Finland proper. About AD 800, probably of Gotland origin. Length about 90 cm. National Museum, Helsinki.

43 Spearheads, *angos*, from western Finland: Vehmaa, Vesilahti, Kokemäki. 600–800 AD. Lengths 49.5, 61.7 and 103 cm. National Museum, Helsinki.

44 Sword pommel of gilt bronze, modelled as a crouching animal; Kirmu-

karmu, Vesilahti, Satakunta. Seventh century AD. Length 6 cm. National Museum, Helsinki.

45 Bronze pendants imitating real bear's teeth, carried as amulets. Viking age. The teeth about 6.8 cm. long. Lehdesmäki, Kalanti, Finland Proper. National Museum, Helsinki.

46 The 'Judge's ring'; Käräjämäki, Eura, Satakunta. Within the stone circle two cremation graves from the seventh century AD. The stone circle was later used to hold court. Diameter 8 m.

47 Bronze chains from Tavastia. About AD 800. National Museum, Helsinki.

48 Burial mounds at Lemböte, Åland.

49 House foundations of the later Iron Age; Storhagen, Finström, Åland. Length 15 m.

50 Reconstruction in miniature of an Åland Iron Age house. After *M. Dreijer*.

51 Clay 'paws' from Åland, found in grave mounds and obviously of magic character. That on the left 11.2 cm. across. National Museum, Helsinki.

52 Inscribed sword-blade: +NNOMNEDMN+ (In nomine Domini) and +AMEN+, apparently made in the Rhineland. Kalanti, Finland proper. Breadth 5.5 cm. National Museum, Helsinki.

53 Eleventh-century spearheads with silvered sockets and decoration in rune-stone style, from western Finland: Mynämäki and Kokemäki. That on the right is 33.5 cm. long, the diameter of the socket 2.8 cm. National Museum, Helsinki.

54 Setting of stones over an inhumation burial of the eleventh century; Tursunperä, Mynämäki, Finland proper.

55 Sword and battle-axe ornamented with inlaid silver threads; Pappilan-

mäki, Eura and Humikkala, Masku. The breadth of the axe-edge 14.5 cm. National Museum, Helsinki.

56   Eleventh-century silver hoard comprising ornaments and coins; Sysmä, Tavastia. The coins are Arabic, Anglo-Saxon and German. Height of the cross 6.9 cm. National Museum, Helsinki.

57   'The lady of Perniö', a reconstruction of west Finnish woman's clothing of about AD 1100, based on grave finds. National Museum, Helsinki.

58   Gold bracelet, found in Metsäpirtti, Karelia. Tenth century. Diameter about 6 cm., weight 73.3 gr. National Museum, Helsinki.

59   Horseshoe-brooch of silver, decorated with Karelian acanthus ornament; Hiitola, Karelia. Breadth 14.9 cm. National Museum, Helsinki.

60   Bronze bird pendant with bells; Tuukkala, Mikkeli, Savo. Tinkling pendants are common in Finno-Ugrian grave finds. Length 5.3 cm. National Museum, Helsinki.

61   Greek Orthodox pendant 'Maria orans' of silver, found in a woman's grave in Kaukola, Karelia. From about AD 1200. Diameter 6 cm. National Museum, Helsinki.

62   Silver cross, showing Christ on one side and the Virgin Mary on the other, found in a man's grave in Taskula, Maaria, Finland proper. Eleventh century. Height 5.6 cm. National Museum, Helsinki.

63   Silver chain of Scandinavian type, with Greek Orthodox crosses, found in a man's grave at Suotniemi, Käkisalmi, Karelia. About AD 1200. Length 73 cm. National Museum, Helsinki.

64   Silver chain with silver pendant, part of a hoard in Kuusamo, north Finland. About AD 1100. Breadth of the pendant 12.2 cm. National Museum, Helsinki.

65   Air photograph of the hill-fort of Vanhalinna near Turku.

66   Offering-stone; Miemala, Vanaja, Tavastia.

Index